THE BIG DISH

RECIPES TO DAZZLE AND AMAZE FROM AMERICA'S MOST SPECTACULAR RESTAURANT

BARTON G. WEISS

PHOTOGRAPHS BY ED ANDERSON

WRITTEN WITH ANGIE MOSIER

RIZZOLI
NEW YORK

New York · Paris · London · Milan

CONTENTS

AND **FOOD** IN LANDSCAPES.

INTRODUCTION

Opportunities for elevated living are available at every moment. Rather than embarking on each day with the hope that something interesting or even thrilling might happen, life can be shifted so that beauty and creativity enter into our lives at each turn. For me, there is no other way to live than to approach my life and my work enthusiastically with open eyes and an open mind to what the possibilities may be.

When I started creating events for celebrations through my company, Barton G., I had a real desire to push the limits beyond what most catering and event design companies were doing. For me, there is never a reason to do what has already been done. The exhilarating challenge is to create drama and theater—devising a different story to pair with each situation and individual. My goal is to inspire people with an experience. Every sense should be activated—not just visual, not just taste—everything. Color, sound, texture, aroma, and the stimulation of feeling as if transported far from anywhere you have ever been.

Over the two decades of work and approximately 20,000 events that my team and I have put together for our clients, we have discovered that no matter what the budget or how big or small a party is, there is always a way to go beyond what might be expected. The trick is not to do something outrageous for the sake of it, but truly to care about the detail and quality of the final presentation. It's also about the freedom of expression that comes from shifting an inclination to do what might seem "appropriate" to asking yourself, "Why not?" There are no rules.

Fantasy and imagination, in the kitchen and on the plate, make every bite—from a passed hors d'oeuvre to a full-on, sweeping buffet—into a realm of sensuality that not only nourishes our bodies, but our spirits as well. The flavor and quality of the food we create for our special event clients has always been the pinnacle of the experience. The idea to open a restaurant where people could have the Barton G. experience every day was the driving force that led us to open three restaurants in Miami and now one in Los Angeles. Guests are treated to drinks and meals that are sophisticated in construction and flavor, yet the food is thought out and delivered with a spirit of real fun and exploration. Hospitality and serving pieces—props, if you will—take each plate to another level, and the opportunity to witness the delightful surprise on customers' faces as dish after extraordinary dish is delivered is part of the experience for diners and staff alike.

But for all of the theatrics, the smoke and mirrors, the exaggerated sizing and playful garnishes, this food is far from a silly gimmick. It involves collaborative brainstorming and deep thought, with sparks of inspiration coming from all parts and people of life. Sometimes I am stimulated by what I have experienced through traveling, while at other times a unique serving piece fires up my imagination. It's important to note that when I say "serving piece," it doesn't usually mean something I have found at a home goods or tabletop store. I've found pieces in toy stores, pet shops, antique markets, and hardware stores. In fact, more often than not, our serving platters and plates are not really platters and plates. Many times, the chefs will come to me with a fantastic idea and we cook and tweak, plate it up and adjust until we come to a fun and delicious outcome that is in the Barton G. style—full of great attention to every detail, especially the taste.

The documentation of our style and recipes has become important to all of us. Barton G.—The Restaurant, is a place where people come to eat great food, served in an extremely novel way. The experience is luxurious but animated and joyful. For us, this book is an archive of the great fun we have had serving and exciting our customers as well as an opportunity to collect some of our favorite recipes into a formal volume. But there is no reason that home cooks can't be inspired to create thrilling experiences for their own friends and family. Over the years, so many people have inquired about our techniques and flavors, and with this book, we hope that readers are encouraged to learn new cooking skills and think outrageously about the entertainment possible at the table.

Rather than following each suggestion to the very last detail, the vignettes and propping ideas more so concern abstract thinking on what being at the table really means. Yes, it's about eating a meal, and yes, it's about having a social interaction, but what if that interaction and the senses that we use at the table are taken to a totally new level? The experience is not just something that has to happen at a special event or at a restaurant—it can be for the everyday. Who says the same joy that takes place at a kid's birthday party can't be for everyone? The scenes and flavors that we have put together here are a great example of the power creativity has to instill pleasure and inventiveness. Creating dishes like these—presenting them to family and guests while witnessing their joy and amusement—is a gift to yourself.

Enjoy this creative and delicious experience—it's the energizing spark that makes what I do so fulfilling.

—BARTON G.

GETTING TOGETHER WITH FRIENDS

IS ALWAYS A CAUSE FOR CELEBRATION.

THE EXTRA-ORDINARY ORDINARY

LOBSTER TRUFFLE MAC & CHEESE

Quite possibly the most decadent combination of ingredients, the Lobster Truffle Mac & Cheese is arguably the most popular item on our menu. You can certainly make individual servings as we have instructed in the recipe, but why not really make a statement by using the lobster shell as a serving dish? By carefully extracting the meat from the cooked lobster, cleaning the shell, and creating openings in the body, claws, and tail with a Dremel tool, you can stuff the shell with the filling, sprinkle with the cheese and bread crumbs, and then give it a final toasting under the broiler. Your centerpiece is the lobster itself!

Serves 4

- 2 (1½-pound) Maine lobsters, cooked
- 3 tablespoons sea salt, plus extra for seasoning
- 1 pound cavatappi pasta

CHEESE SAUCE
- 3 tablespoons unsalted butter
- ½ cup all-purpose flour
- 1 cup lobster or fish stock
- 2 cups milk
- 1 cup heavy whipping cream
- ½ teaspoon freshly grated nutmeg
- 2 cups shredded Gruyère cheese
- 2 cups shredded white cheddar cheese
- 2 cups shredded Colby Jack cheese
- 1 tablespoon truffle oil
- 2 tablespoons chopped canned black truffles
- Freshly ground black pepper

Remove the meat from the claws and tail of the lobsters. Cut the meat into 1-inch chunks.

Bring 5 quarts of water and the 3 tablespoons sea salt to a boil in a large pot. Add the pasta and cook for 7 minutes or until al dente. Drain and set aside.

For the cheese sauce:
In a large, heavy saucepan set over medium-low heat, melt the butter. Add the flour and whisk for 1 minute. Increase the heat to medium-high, add the stock, milk, and cream and whisk until smooth. Continue cooking for 5 minutes or until the sauce has thickened. Add the nutmeg and whisk to combine.

Remove from the heat and add the Gruyère, white cheddar, and Colby Jack cheeses and stir until melted and smooth. Add the cooked pasta and stir to combine. Add the lobster meat, truffle oil, and chopped truffles. Taste and season with salt and pepper, if needed. Divide the mixture among 4 individual, oven-safe, casserole dishes or transfer to one large dish (or a well-cleaned lobster shell—see headnote) for a family-size portion.

Preheat the broiler.

continued

BREAD CRUMB TOPPING

- **4 tablespoons (½ stick) unsalted butter**
- **1 cup panko bread crumbs**
- **1 tablespoon chopped fresh flat-leaf parsley**
- **1 tablespoon chopped fresh tarragon**
- **½ teaspoon sea salt**
- **½ cup shredded sharp yellow cheddar cheese**

For the bread crumb topping:

Melt the butter in a sauté pan over medium heat. Add the bread crumbs and toss until golden. Strain through a fine-mesh strainer, transfer the breadcrumbs to a paper towel–lined plate, and spread to cool. Combine the cooled bread crumbs with the parsley, tarragon, and sea salt.

Top the casseroles with the shredded yellow cheese and sprinkle with the bread crumb mixture.

Broil the casseroles for 2 minutes or until the cheese is melted and the breadcrumbs are a deep golden brown. Cool slightly before serving.

BOXED LUNCH SANDWICHES

Tiny sandwiches may be the perfect party food. They are easy to pick up and eat in one bite and they allow guests to try more than one flavor without filling up too fast. I also like to think beyond the "passed tray" approach to serving appetizers, and when it comes to sandwiches, there are definitely no boundaries. Collections of wooden, glass, and cigar boxes can contain the "boxed lunch" and they can be placed on coffee tables and credenzas for a party at home.

Another idea is to individually skewer sandwiches onto forks for an alternative presentation that is easy to pick up. Our team made some really cool "tool" forks by removing the metal tool part of screwdrivers and replacing them with forks so that the forks have handles like a screwdriver.

MINI CLUB SANDWICHES

Serves 4

- **3 slices toasted white bread**
- **2 ounces roasted, sliced turkey breast**
- **1 recipe Avocado Mayonnaise (page 22)**
- **4 strips cooked bacon**
- **1 Roma tomato, sliced**
- **2 leaves baby romaine lettuce**

Place the toasted bread slices on a work surface. Spread the Avocado Mayonnaise on one slice, then top with half of the turkey slices, 2 strips of the bacon, half of the tomato slices, and 1 baby romaine leaf. Spread some of the Avocado Mayonnaise on the second toasted bread slice and place atop the sandwich, mayonnaise side up. Layer the remaining ingredients atop the bread, ending with the romaine and the third slice of toast. You should end up with a double stack of ingredients with bread in the middle. Using a serrated knife, cut the sandwich into quarters. Skewer each piece with a toothpick and serve.

continued

AVOCADO MAYONNAISE

about 2 cups

- **1 ripe avocado, pitted and peeled**
- **1 cup mayonnaise**
- **1 tablespoon freshly squeezed lime juice**
- **2 teaspoons chopped fresh chives**
- **Kosher salt**
- **Freshly ground black pepper**

In a small mixing bowl, mash the avocado with a fork. Add the mayonnaise, lime juice, and chives and stir to combine. Season as desired with salt and pepper. Use immediately or cover and chill for up to 2 days.

MINI GRILLED CHEESE

Serves 4

- **4 (½-inch-thick) slices brioche**
- **4 ounces Brie, Saint André, or other triple cream cheese, at room temperature**
- **1 tablespoon white truffle oil**
- **Kosher salt**
- **Freshly ground black pepper**
- **1 tablespoon unsalted butter**

Place 2 slices of the brioche in the microwave for 10 to 15 seconds or until very soft and spongy. Spread half of the cheese onto one slice of the bread, drizzle with half of the truffle oil and season with salt and pepper. Top with the second piece of bread. Use the blunt side of a 2-inch round cookie cutter as a sandwich cutter to create a round, ravioli-shaped sandwich. Press down on the edges of the sandwich to make sure they are sealed. Repeat with the remaining ingredients to make second sandwich.

Melt the butter in a sauté pan over medium heat and cook sandwiches until they are golden brown on both sides, 2 to 3 minutes per side. Slice in half and serve warm.

MINI LOBSTER AND SHRIMP ROLLS

Serves 4

- **2 tablespoons crème fraîche**
- **2 tablespoons mayonnaise**
- **1 tablespoon confectioners' sugar**
- **2 teaspoons rice wine vinegar**
- **1½ teaspoons Pernod**
- **1 tablespoon chopped fresh dill, plus extra sprigs for garnish**
- **Kosher salt**
- **2 ounces cooked lobster meat, coarsely chopped**
- **2 ounces cooked shrimp, coarsely chopped**
- **4 (1½-inch-thick) slices baguette, toasted and sliced through the center three-quarters of the way through to make a mini bun**
- **4 grape tomatoes, halved**
- **Fresh chive tips, for garnish**

In a mixing bowl, whisk together the crème fraiche, mayonnaise, confectioners' sugar, vinegar, Pernod, and chopped dill. Taste and season with salt as desired. Add the lobster meat and shrimp and stir to combine. Spoon the mixture into the toasted baguette "rolls" and top with the dill sprigs, tomatoes, and chive tips.

MINI HOTDOGS

Serves 4

- **4 cocktail-size smoked sausages ("little smokies"), heated**
- **4 (1½-inch-thick) slices baguette, toasted and sliced through the center three-quarters of the way through to make a mini bun**
- **Yellow mustard**
- **Ketchup**
- **Green relish**

Place a sausage in the center of each baguette "roll" and garnish with mustard, ketchup, and relish.

Serve on the ends of forks or in a decorative box with a lid.

TOASTER PASTRY "BAR-TON BLEU"

Chicken cordon bleu meets toaster pastry in a sophisticated take on classic and comforting dishes. At Barton G.—The Restaurant, these savory tarts are filled and baked to perfection, and served in a retro toaster that is brought to the table. You could do the same or make a fun centerpiece, using a toaster and then stacking the rest of the pastries around the toaster.

Serves 6

TOASTED PASTRY
- **6 boneless, skinless chicken breasts**
- **1 teaspoon garlic powder**
- **6 slices prosciutto**
- **6 slices provolone cheese**
- **¾ cup crumbled goat cheese**
- **¾ cup grated Gruyère cheese (about 8 ounces)**
- **6 (7 x 7-inch) frozen puff pastry sheets**
- **4 tablespoons butter, melted**

"BAR-TON BLEU" DIP
- **1¼ cups mayonnaise**
- **¼ cup grated Parmesan cheese**
- **2 tablespoons freshly squeezed lemon juice**
- **2 teaspoons Worcestershire sauce**
- **3 tablespoons chopped fresh herbs, such as a mixture of oregano and parsley**
- **Pinch of chili powder**

For the pastry:
On a work surface, place the chicken breasts between sheets of plastic wrap and pound to ¼-inch thickness. Split each breast widthwise and trim a little off of each end, creating a square. Season each breast with garlic powder and lay a piece of prosciutto on top of one side of each breast. Top with a slice of provolone. Sprinkle with the goat cheese and Gruyère, dividing them equally. Fold the empty side of the breast over to create a square pouch. Refrigerate for 1 hour.

Preheat oven to 350°F. Line a rimmed baking sheet with parchment paper.

Arrange the puff pastry sheets on a lightly floured work surface. Brush the edges with melted butter. Place a chicken-and-cheese parcel in the center of each square. Fold the sides of sheet over to cover filling. Brush again with butter, then fold both ends over. Brush the tops of each package with melted butter. Set the pastries on the prepared baking sheet and bake for 10 to 15 minutes, until the internal temperature of the chicken reaches 165°F. Remove from the oven and cool for 10 minutes before serving with the dip.

For the dip:
Stir together all the ingredients for the dip in a small bowl and refrigerate until ready to use.

continued

AT THE
TABLE,
AS IN LIFE,
PRESENTATION
IS
EVERYTHING.

BASS IN BAGS

Cooking fish en papillote, or in parchment, is a great way to steam in flavor. A paper lunch bag achieves the same result. When sealed with a clothespin and personalized with the diner's name written on the outside, it becomes the ultimate sack lunch. The inspiration for this was a brown-bag lunch in the garden; it's fun to line up a few of them for your friends to find their names and tear into the bags for a delicious and healthful meal.

Note: To create our garden scene, you will need 12 paper lunch bags, 12 clothespins (to seal the bags), and a roll of waxed paper. You can also use a marker to put individual names on each bag or write what each bag contains on the outside. You can make the miso "edible soil," which is essentially our version of deeply flavored bread crumbs for serving with the fish and potatoes, up to a week ahead of serving.

Serves 6

BASS AND VEGETABLES

- **2 tablespoons olive oil, divided**
- **6 (6-ounce) sea bass fillets, pin bones removed**
- **Sea salt**
- **Freshly ground black pepper**
- **2 tablespoons unsalted butter, divided**
- **6 thin lemon slices**
- **2 carrots, julienned**
- **1 leek, white and green parts only, julienned**
- **2 celery ribs, julienned**
- **1 small zucchini, julienned**

ROASTED POTATOES

- **1½ pounds peewee potatoes (such as peewee fingerling or Baby Yellow Dutch potatoes)**
- **1 tablespoon lemon zest**
- **1 tablespoon freshly squeezed lemon juice**
- **1 tablespoon olive oil**
- **½ teaspoon sea salt**
- **¼ teaspoon freshly ground black pepper**

Preheat the oven to 375°F. Line a large rimmed baking sheet with parchment paper.

Make the bass and vegetables:
Heat 1 tablespoon of the olive oil in a large sauté pan over medium-high heat until it shimmers. Season each fillet with salt and pepper and sear 3 sea bass fillets at a time, flesh-side down, for 1 to 2 minutes or until light golden brown. Remove to a paper towel–lined platter and repeat with the remaining tablespoon olive oil and 3 sea bass fillets.

Line the bottom of 6 paper lunch bags with a piece of waxed paper.

Place a sea bass fillet in each bag and top each with a teaspoon of butter, a lemon slice, and a mixture of the julienned vegetables. Fold over the tops of the bags and clip each with a clothespin.

Make the potatoes:
In a large mixing bowl, toss the potatoes with the lemon zest, lemon juice, olive oil, salt, and pepper. Divide the potatoes among 6 paper lunch bags. Fold over the tops of the bags and clip each with a clothespin.

continued

MISO EDIBLE SOIL

- **¾ cup white miso paste**
- **¼ cup mixed nuts**
- **3 thin slices black bread or pumper-nickel**
- **1 cup dried portobello mushrooms**
- **3 tablespoons dark brown sugar**
- **½ cup dark raisins**
- **1 tablespoon black olive paste (tapenade)**
- **Olive oil (optional)**

Place the potato bags and fish bags on the prepared baking sheet and cook for 20 minutes, until the fish is just cooked through.

To serve, spread the "edible soil" on a serving tray or wooden board. You can decorate with garden tools or gloves if you like. Arrange the cooked fish and potatoes in their paper bags directly on your prepared gardenscape.

Make the miso edible soil:
Preheat the oven to 150°F.

Place the white miso paste between 2 sheets of parchment paper and roll it out into a thin, even layer. Remove the top layer of parchment paper. Transfer the bottom piece of parchment paper with the miso on it to a baking sheet and bake for 2 to 3 hours or until completely dry. Remove from the oven and let cool at room temperature; increase the oven temperature to 250°F. Once cool, transfer the dried miso to a food processor and pulse until powdered. Store at room temperature in an airtight container until ready to use.

Spread the mixed nuts and bread slices on a rimmed baking sheet and bake for 30 minutes or until crisp. Cool completely and transfer to the bowl of a food processor. Add the mushrooms, brown sugar, and raisins and pulse until coarsely chopped. Add the miso powder and olive paste and pulse again, just until blended. Do not overwork or it will turn muddy. If you prefer a more soil-like texture, add a few drops of olive oil. Store this mixture at room temperature until ready to use. If you are holding it for more than 8 hours, transfer to an airtight container and store in the refrigerator for up to 1 week.

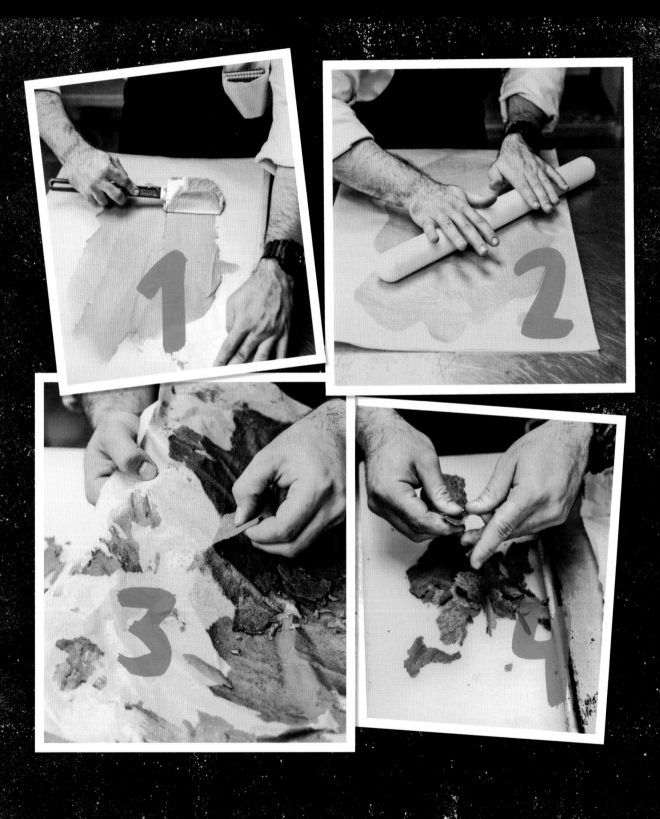

SHEPHERD'S PIE PARFAITS

Serving savory food in clear dessert bowls or cocktail glasses is a gorgeous way to highlight the layers of flavor within. Shepherd's pie is one of the great comfort foods of all time but rarely seen in an elegant presentation. We've used different types of potatoes and spinach to create colorful layers with the meat filling. Vegetable garnishes top off the "parfaits." Try this technique with your kids—it's a great way to get them to eat their vegetables.

Note: *The meat mixtures in this dish are even better if made a day ahead of time, to allow the flavors to meld. Cover and chill them separately in the refrigerator, then reheat them when you are ready to assemble and serve the parfaits.*

You can also make the most of the time required to bake the potatoes by either cooking the meat mixtures (if you didn't do it ahead of time) or preparing your garnishes.

Serves 8

POTATOES

YUKON GOLD

- **2½ pounds Yukon Gold potatoes**
- **1½ cups heavy whipping cream, at room temperature**
- **½ cup (1 stick) unsalted butter, at room temperature**
- **1 teaspoon kosher salt**

PURPLE

- **1½ pounds purple potatoes**
- **1 cup heavy whipping cream, at room temperature**
- **1 teaspoon kosher salt**

For the potatoes:
Preheat the oven to 375°F.

Place all the potatoes (Yukon gold, purple, and sweet potatoes) on 2 rimmed baking sheets and bake in the oven until they are tender and cooked through, about 1 hour. Remove from the oven and cool.

When cool enough to handle, scoop out the potato flesh and discard the peels. Keeping the varieties of potatoes separate, pass the potatoes, one variety at a time, through a ricer into a separate mixing bowl or mash very well. Add the butter, heavy cream, and seasonings in the quantities indicated for each variety and mash or whisk together to create a smooth mixture. Keep warm.

continued

yukon gold
potatoes

sweet
potatoes

purple
potatoes

SWEET POTATO

- 1½ pounds sweet potatoes
- ½ cup heavy whipping cream, at room temperature
- 4 tablespoons (½ stick) unsalted butter, at room temperature
- 2 teaspoons light brown sugar
- 1 teaspoon kosher salt
- ¼ teaspoon ground cinnamon

SPINACH

- 1 (16-ounce) package frozen spinach, thawed and squeezed to remove all liquid

MEAT

BEEF

- 1 tablespoon canola oil
- 1 small onion, diced
- 1 pound ground beef
- 2 sprigs fresh thyme
- 1 bay leaf
- ¾ cup beef broth
- 1 tablespoon tomato paste
- 1 tablespoon Worcestershire sauce
- 1 tablespoon hot sauce, such as Tabasco
- ½ teaspoon kosher salt
- ¼ teaspoon freshly ground black pepper

For the spinach:
Preheat the oven to 300°F. Line a rimmed baking sheet with parchment paper.

Evenly spread the squeezed-out spinach on the prepared baking sheet and bake for 5 minutes. Toss and bake for 5 minutes more. The spinach should be almost dry, but not crispy.

For the meat:
Prepare all three meat mixtures according to the directions below, in separate sauté pans. Once completed, hold in a warm place or even better, store in the refrigerator overnight to allow the flavors to meld, and reheat when ready to use.

While the potatoes are baking, place the oil in large skillet or sauté pan and set over medium-high heat. Once the oil shimmers, add the onion and cook until translucent. Add the meat and herbs and cook, stirring frequently, until the fat is rendered and the meat has browned, 4 to 5 minutes.

Transfer the mixture to a fine-mesh strainer and press with the back of a large spoon or ladle to remove the fat. Return the meat mixture to the pan and add the beef broth and seasonings and stir to combine. Reduce the heat to low and cook for 5 minutes. Transfer to a container and keep warm.

LAMB

- **1 tablespoon canola oil**
- **1 small onion, diced**
- **1 pound ground lamb**
- **1 sprig fresh rosemary**
- **1 bay leaf**
- **¾ cup beef broth**
- **1 tablespoon Dijon mustard**
- **½ teaspoon kosher salt**
- **¼ teaspoon freshly ground black pepper**

PORK

- **1 tablespoon canola oil**
- **1 small onion, diced**
- **1 pound ground pork**
- **2 sprigs fresh thyme**
- **1 bay leaf**
- **3 ounces beef broth**
- **2 ounces barbecue sauce**
- **1 ounce Worcestershire sauce**
- **1 tablespoon hot sauce, such as Tabasco**
- **½ teaspoon kosher salt**
- **¼ teaspoon freshly ground black pepper**

GARNISHES

- **Roasted grape tomatoes**
- **Chopped fresh herbs**
- **Green peas**
- **Steamed broccoli florets**
- **Shredded cheddar cheese**
- **Green onions**

To assemble and serve:

Combine the spinach and one-third of the Yukon Gold potato mixture together in the bowl of a food processor. Pulse 6 to 8 times to create a green potato purée. Keep warm.

Using 12-ounce parfait glasses, build the dish with alternate layers of meat and potatoes, creating a variety of colors and textures in each glass. Play with the combinations and layers as you like, topping with any of the suggested vegetable garnishes; you can even assemble each "parfait" to look like a fancy, savory version of a sundae.

LOBSTER TATER TOTS

I love taking a homey everyday recipe and turning it into something special. In this recipe, lobster—the ultimate luxury seafood—is mixed with humbler ingredients—cheese, chives, and potatoes—and deep-fried like a potato croquette. You can serve these in little paper trays or cones or give them the VIP treatment in a shining silver serving compote.

Serves 6

- 2 pounds russet potatoes, peeled and baked at 350°F for 1 hour (potatoes will not be completely cooked)
- ¾ cup sour cream
- ¾ cup shredded Swiss cheese (about 6 ounces)
- 1 tablespoon lobster base (available online, in specialty stores, or the sauce section of your grocery)
- Pinch of freshly ground black pepper
- 1 cup diced cooked lobster meat
- 2 tablespoons minced fresh chives
- ¾ cup instant potato flakes, divided
- 3 tablespoons all-purpose flour
- 1 whole egg, beaten with 1 teaspoon water
- 2 quarts peanut oil
- Sea salt
- Orange Chili Sauce (recipe follows), for serving
- "Bar-ton Bleu" Dip (page 25), for serving

ORANGE CHILI SAUCE

- 1 cup orange marmalade, puréed until smooth
- 1 tablespoon Thai chili sauce

Allow the baked potatoes to cool completely. Grate them into a large bowl using a box grater. In a separate bowl, combine the sour cream, shredded cheese, lobster base, and black pepper. Add the sour cream mixture to the grated potatoes. Stir in the lobster meat, chives, and ¼ cup of the potato flakes and mix well.

Put the remaining ½ cup potato flakes, flour, and beaten whole egg in 3 separate bowls. Using about 3 tablespoons for each tot, shape the mixture into small cylinders. You can use a ring mold or your hands. (You should have a total of about 24 tots.) Roll each cylinder in the flour, then the egg, and then in the potato flakes.

Heat the oil in a 5-quart Dutch oven set over high heat until it reaches 350°F. Fry the tots in batches (a few at a time) until golden. Using a slotted spoon, transfer the tots to a paper towel–lined plate to drain. Season with sea salt and serve immediately in a basket with Orange Chili Sauce and "Bar-ton Bleu" Dip on the side.

For the chili sauce:
Combine the marmalade and chili sauce in a small bowl and stir to combine.

continued

VOODOO SHRIMP

The flavors and spirit of New Orleans inspired this recipe and presentation. The slightly spicy Cajun style of the filling for the shrimp includes both blackened seasoning and filé powder. Filé is the traditional thickener for gumbo; made from the dried and ground leaves of the sassafras tree, it has a distinctive flavor. For our "voodoo" presentation, we like to serve the skewers in a sturdy, tapered glass vase so that the shrimp are at the top, coming out of the vase, skewer-end down. Placing a small chunk of dry ice and a bit of hot water in the base just before serving creates a mysterious fog.

Note: *You'll need twelve 10-inch-long wooden skewers for the shrimp. You can make the cocktail sauce up to 2 days ahead of time and keep it chilled in the fridge.*

Makes 12

SHRIMP AND JAMBALAYA STUFFING
- **20 jumbo shrimp**
- **1 tablespoon vegetable oil**
- **2 tablespoons diced red bell pepper**
- **¼ cup sliced green onions**
- **¼ cup diced yellow squash**
- **2 garlic cloves, minced**
- **½ teaspoon filé powder (also called gumbo filé; available online and in specialty markets)**
- **½ teaspoon blackened seasoning (such as Paul Prudhomme's Blackened Redfish Magic)**
- **Salt**
- **½ cup cooked brown rice**
- **¾ cup lump crabmeat**
- **1 egg white, lightly beaten**

For the shrimp and stuffing:
Peel and remove the tails from 8 of the shrimp. Devein the shrimp and set aside. Peel the remaining 12 shrimp, leaving the tail intact. Devein the shrimp and butterfly by inserting a paring knife into the top, head region of the shrimp and making a slice down the back, all the way to the tail, making sure not to slice all the way through. Rinse the shrimp in cold water and use your fingers to open and flatten the shrimp. Place the butterflied shrimp on a tray or plate and set aside.

Heat the oil in a sauté pan over medium-high heat. Add the bell pepper, green onion, squash, and garlic and sauté until they begin to sweat and soften just a bit, about 3 minutes. Season with the filé powder, blackened seasoning, and salt. Remove from the heat and set aside to cool.

Add the 8 reserved peeled shrimp to the bowl of a food processor and purée to create a paste. Transfer the paste to a mixing bowl and add the cooled cooked vegetables, cooked rice, crabmeat, and beaten egg white and fold gently to mix.

continued

TO ASSEMBLE

- **Salt**
- **12 pastry spring roll wrappers (not rice paper)**
- **2 eggs, lightly beaten with 1 teaspoon water**
- **1 cup coconut flakes**
- **¼ cup sesame seeds**
- **6 to 8 cups vegetable oil, for frying**

PINEAPPLE-COCONUT COCKTAIL SAUCE

- **½ cup canned diced pineapple with juice**
- **⅓ cup coconut milk**
- **⅓ cup chili sauce (such as Heinz)**
- **2 tablespoons cream of coconut (such as Coco Lopez)**
- **2 tablespoons prepared horseradish**
- **1 teaspoon Sriracha hot sauce**
- **Pinch of salt**

To assemble the skewers:

Place the 12 butterflied shrimp on a work surface, cut-side up. Sprinkle the shrimp with salt and spoon 1 to 2 tablespoons of the stuffing mixture onto each shrimp. Fold over, cover, and refrigerate until ready to use.

Skewer each of the stuffed shrimp lengthwise from tail to head without going all the way through the head. Cut the spring roll wrappers in half lengthwise and lay 6 strips on a work surface. Brush the length of each wrapper with the egg wash and lay a skewered, stuffed shrimp sideways across and toward the end of the wrapper. The shrimp should be lying across the pastry strip with the skewer coming out of the tail end. Begin rolling the pastry around the shrimp to cover all of the meat with a bit of the tail exposed, to create a tight spring roll. In a shallow dish, combine the coconut and sesame seeds. Brush the rolled shrimp with more of the egg wash and then roll them in the coconut and sesame seeds.

In a medium- to- large saucepan set over medium-high heat, heat the vegetable oil to 350°F. Carefully fry the skewered shrimp until they are golden brown and set on a plate or tray lined with paper towels to drain. Serve hot with the Pineapple-Coconut Cocktail Sauce.

For the cocktail sauce:

Place all of the ingredients in a food processor or blender and blend just until combined. You can make it as chunky or smooth as you like. Cover and chill in the refrigerator until ready to use, up to 2 days.

THERE'S NO REASON WHY YOU HAVE TO

fried
sesame balls

green tea
macarons

praline
egg rolls

peach-
blueberry
egg rolls

DIM SUM DESSERTS

When a dim sum cart rattles past your table at a Chinese restaurant, the smells, sights, and sounds of the experience all work together to tempt you to choose just one more dish. Who can resist the bite-size dumplings and fried morsels in their tiny bamboo boxes and mats? The same goes for these delectable sweets, arranged together as a buffet of diminutive desserts.

Note: *To assemble the sweets for serving, use small bamboo steamer baskets (available in Asian and international markets and online) to hold the various macarons, sesame seed balls, and egg rolls. Pour sauces into small stainless-steel dipping sauce containers and offer chopsticks for your guests to use to pick up their sweets.*

FRIED SESAME SEED BALLS

Makes 8 to 10 pieces

- ½ cup white sesame seeds
- ¼ cup confectioners' sugar
- 1 cup all-purpose flour
- 2 tablespoons granulated sugar
- 3 large eggs, beaten
- 1 teaspoon vanilla extract
- ¼ cup cornstarch
- 1 quart vegetable oil, for deep-frying

Preheat the oven to 300°F. Spread the sesame seeds on a baking sheet lined with parchment paper and toast in the oven until light brown, about 20 minutes. Remove from the oven and let cool. Transfer the toasted sesame seeds to a bowl and add the confectioners' sugar. Stir to combine and set aside.

In a medium mixing bowl, combine the flour with the granulated sugar. Stir in ½ cup water, add the beaten eggs, and mix until smooth.

In a medium saucepan set over medium-high heat, bring 1 cup water to a boil. Add the flour mixture and stir vigorously over medium heat until it thickens, 1 to 2 minutes. Add the vanilla and stir well. Pour the mixture into a greased 8-inch-square Pyrex dish. Pat with your hand to ½-inch thickness and transfer to the refrigerator to chill for about 1 hour.

Use your hands or a small ice-cream scoop to scoop out the chilled mixture. Roll into 1-inch balls. Dredge the balls in the cornstarch.

In a frying pan, heat the oil to about 340°F. Fry the balls, a few at a time, for about 3 minutes or until light brown. As soon as they get brown, use a strainer to transfer the balls to a plate and sprinkle with the sesame seed mixture.

GREEN TEA MACARONS WITH MATCHA GANACHE

Makes 8 to 10 macarons

- 1¼ cups confectioners' sugar
- 1½ cups almond flour
- 2 tablespoons cooking-grade matcha green tea powder, divided
- 3 large egg whites
- Pinch of table salt
- ¼ cup granulated sugar
- ¼ cup heavy whipping cream
- 6 ounces white chocolate, finely chopped

For the macaron cookies:
Preheat the oven to 200°F.

In a large mixing bowl, sift together the confectioners' sugar, almond flour, and 1 tablespoon of the green tea powder. Set aside.

Line 2 baking sheets with parchment paper or silicone baking mats. To make uniformly sized cookies, mark circles on the parchment or baking mats using a 1½-inch cutter dipped in flour.

In the bowl of a stand mixer fitted with the whisk attachment, beat the egg whites on medium speed until foamy. Add the salt and gradually add the granulated sugar and beat until medium-soft peaks form.

Using a rubber spatula, fold half of the almond flour mixture into the egg white mixture until just incorporated. Fold in the remaining almond mixture and then firmly tap the bottom of the bowl on the counter to eliminate air pockets.

Transfer the mixture to a pastry bag fitted with a ½-inch plain round tip. Pipe the mixture into the circles marked on the prepared baking sheets.

Transfer to the oven and bake, rotating the baking sheets halfway through, until the macarons are slightly firm and can be gently lifted off the parchment (the bottoms will be dry), 20 to 25 minutes. Let the macarons cool on the baking sheets for 5 minutes before transferring to a wire rack to cool completely.

For the matcha ganache:
Place the white chocolate in a heatproof bowl and set aside. In a medium saucepan, combine the heavy cream and remaining 1 tablespoon green tea powder and heat over medium-low heat until just boiling. Immediately pour the hot cream mixture over the chopped chocolate and stir until smooth. Allow the ganache to cool slightly in the bowl, stirring occasionally to keep it creamy.

To assemble the macarons:
Transfer the ganache to a pastry bag fitted with a plain round piping tip. Pipe some ganache onto the bottom of one macaron cookie and top with the flat side of another macaron cookie, pressing slightly to adhere and form a sandwich. Repeat with remaining ganache and macaron cookies.

PEACH-BLUEBERRY EGG ROLLS

Makes 4 egg rolls

- 1½ tablespoons granulated sugar
- ¼ teaspoon ground cinnamon
- 1 teaspoon arrowroot starch
- 1 peach, peeled, seeded, and chopped
- ½ cup fresh blueberries
- ¼ teaspoon lemon zest
- 1 teaspoon lemon juice
- 3 tablespoons unsalted butter, at room temperature, divided
- 4 egg roll wrappers
- 4 to 6 cups canola oil, for frying
- ¼ cup confectioners' sugar

In a large mixing bowl, mix together the granulated sugar, cinnamon, and arrowroot starch. Add the peach, blueberries, lemon zest and juice, and toss together to coat.

Place an egg roll wrapper on a work surface. Spoon 2 tablespoons of the peach-blueberry mixture onto the wrapper and dot with about 1 teaspoon of the butter. Roll the wrapper into an egg roll shape and seal the edges with a little bit of water.

Add just enough canola oil to a nonstick skillet to coat the bottom and place over medium heat. Place the fruit-filled egg rolls in the pan and cook for a minute or two, turning, until they are brown and crispy. Transfer the egg rolls to a plate lined with a paper towel to absorb excess oil. Dust the egg rolls with confectioners' sugar and cut each roll in half on a bias.

CHOCOLATE-COVERED HAZELNUT PRALINE EGG ROLLS

Makes 4 egg rolls

EGG ROLLS
- 4 egg roll wrappers
- 2 bananas, thinly sliced
- 5 ounces good-quality semisweet chocolate, shaved, plus 6 ounces semisweet chocolate, melted
- Ground cinnamon
- ⅓ cup vegetable oil

HAZELNUT PRALINE
- Vegetable oil cooking spray
- ½ cup granulated sugar
- 1 teaspoon light corn syrup
- Pinch of salt
- ⅓ cup hazelnuts, toasted, skins rubbed off with a damp cloth

CHOCOLATE SAUCE
- ⅔ cup unsweetened cocoa powder
- 1⅔ cups granulated sugar
- 1 teaspoon vanilla extract

For the egg rolls:
Place the egg roll wrappers on a work surface. Place 6 banana slices, 1 table-spoon of shaved chocolate, and a dash of cinnamon in the center of each egg roll wrapper. Tuck the ends over the filling and roll up the wrapper. Heat the vegetable oil in a medium saucepan over medium-high heat. When almost smoking, drop the egg rolls carefully into the oil. You must turn them quickly on all sides because they will brown very quickly. When brown, remove them from the pan and drain on a paper towel to absorb excess oil.

For the hazelnut praline:
Preheat the oven to 350°F. Coat a rimmed baking sheet with cooking spray. In a small saucepan set over medium-high heat, combine the sugar, corn syrup, salt, and 1 tablespoon water and cook, stirring constantly, until the sugar dissolves. Continue to cook, without stirring, until the sugar mixture reaches a deep amber color, about 10 minutes. Remove from the heat, stir in the nuts, and spread evenly on the prepared baking sheet. Transfer to the oven and bake for about 30 minutes. Transfer to a wire rack to cool completely. When completely cool, break the praline into medium pieces and transfer to a resealable plastic bag. Using a rolling pin, crush the praline into small pieces.

For the chocolate sauce:
In a medium saucepan over medium heat, combine the cocoa powder, sugar, and 1¼ cups water. Bring to a boil and let boil for 1 minute. Remove from the heat and stir in the vanilla. Allow the sauce to cool slightly.

To assemble and serve:
Coat the egg rolls in melted chocolate and immediately sprinkle with the praline crumbles. When the chocolate has set, use a sharp knife to cut each roll in half, on the bias. Serve the sauce on the side for dipping.

mint "ranch"

wing fritters

marzipan celery sticks

CHICKENLESS WINGS

Here's a sweet dessert version of the popular happy-hour snack. It's a basket of wing-shaped fried dough fritters (much like the funnel cakes you might find at a fair) tossed in a honey-orange marmalade "wing sauce" and served with a cool "ranch" mint-and-chocolate-flecked whipped cream. We also like to pair it with celery stalks made from marzipan tinted green. In fact, this is exactly the kind of wacky recipe that you could imagine being served at a summer festival or from a food truck.

Makes about 12 "wings"

SPECIAL EQUIPMENT:
- **large pastry bag**
- **medium-size flat piping tip (available at cooking supply stores)**

WING FRITTERS
- **1¼ cups all-purpose flour**
- **3 tablespoons granulated sugar**
- **2¾ teaspoons baking powder**
- **¼ teaspoon ground cinnamon**
- **¼ teaspoon table salt**
- **1 large egg**
- **1 cup milk**
- **2 tablespoons unsalted butter, melted**
- **2 cups vegetable oil, for frying (more if needed for the size of your pan)**
- **1 cup orange marmalade**
- **½ cup honey**
- **½ teaspoon yellow food coloring**
- **½ teaspoon orange food coloring**

For the wing fritters:

In a medium mixing bowl, combine the flour, sugar, baking powder, cinnamon, and salt. In a separate small bowl, beat the egg slightly and then blend in the milk and melted butter. Add the egg mixture to the dry ingredients and stir with a whisk until blended. Pour the batter into a pastry bag fitted with a medium-size flat piping tip.

Pour 1 inch of oil into a frying pan set over medium-high heat. When the oil is hot (about 340°F), carefully pipe the batter into the oil, creating wing-like shapes. Fry until golden brown and crispy on the outside. Using a slotted spoon, remove each "wing" and drain on a plate lined with paper towels to absorb excess oil. Set aside.

In a saucepan set over medium heat, warm the orange jam and honey together until they are melted and soft, about 3 minutes. Add the yellow and orange food coloring until you get the desired "wing sauce" color. Keep warm until you are ready to toss the wing fritters in the glaze.

continued

MINT "RANCH" CHANTILLY CREAM

- **1 cup heavy whipping cream**
- **¼ cup confectioners' sugar**
- **2 tablespoons chopped fresh mint**
- **¼ cup finely chopped semisweet chocolate**

For the mint "ranch" cream:

In the bowl of a stand mixer fitted with the whisk attachment, whip together the heavy cream and confectioners' sugar until soft peaks form. Fold in the chopped mint and chocolate and refrigerate for up to 1 hour until ready to serve.

To serve:

To glaze the wings, place the fritters in a large bowl, pour the warm glaze over the fritters, and very gently toss until each fritter is coated with the glaze. Place the fritter wings in a basket or other creative serving dish with a side of the mint "ranch" cream for dipping.

2

2 A DOUBLE-TAKE ON THE PLATE

THE CHICKEN AND THE EGG

Which came first, we'll never know, but who cares when they can be combined to make this playful barnyard collection of snacks? Deviled eggs and chicken wings are two iconic appetizers and when served together in this way, each person gets a little of both. Save your egg cartons or go out and find some pretty ceramic ones and use a combination of both.

Serves 10

SPECIAL EQUIPMENT

- **10 decorative ceramic egg cartons (available online or at home décor stores) with 6 spaces for eggs, or cardboard egg cartons (either the 6-egg size or the dozen-egg size cut in half) with lids removed to make open serving cartons**
- **10 clean eggshell halves (you can save eggshells, wash them out, and keep them indefinitely), or 10 eggcups or small condiment bowls**

WINGS

- **1½ cups all-purpose flour**
- **¼ teaspoon poultry seasoning**
- **¼ teaspoon ground paprika**
- **¼ teaspoon garlic powder**
- **¼ teaspoon onion powder**
- **Pinch of ground white pepper**
- **Pinch of kosher salt**
- **30 chicken wing drummettes**
- **1½ cups canola oil**
- **Hot sauce, such as Tabasco**

For the wings:
Preheat the oven to 200°F.

Combine the flour and all seasonings in a large mixing bowl.

On each of the drummettes, make an incision through the skin all the way around the thinner end of the bone. Grab the skin with a kitchen towel and pull toward the fatter end of the bone where most of the meat is located. Push all the meat and skin toward this end, exposing clean bone. Toss the wings in the seasoned flour and set aside.

Heat the oil to 360°F in a large Dutch oven. Fry the wings, in several batches, for 6 to 8 minutes or until golden brown and cooked through. Transfer to a paper towel–lined rimmed baking sheet and hold in the oven until ready to serve.

continued

COUNTRY EGGS

- **20 hard-boiled eggs**
- **2 tablespoons Dijon mustard**
- **1 tablespoon mayonnaise**

BLUE CHEESE DRESSING

- **½ cup crumbled blue cheese**
- **⅓ cup buttermilk**
- **2 tablespoons Dijon mustard**
- **2 tablespoons mayonnaise**
- **Salt**
- **Freshly ground black pepper**

GARNISHES

- **Cherry tomatoes**
- **Pickled okra**
- **Carrot sticks**
- **Celery sticks**
- **Radishes**

For the eggs:
Carefully peel the hard-boiled eggs and rinse to make sure any remaining shell bits are removed. Cut off top third (the narrow end) of each hard-boiled egg. Remove the yolk from each egg and transfer the yolks to a mixing bowl. Using a fork, mash the yolks. Add the mustard and mayonnaise and combine until smooth. Season with salt and pepper to taste. Transfer the mixture to a piping bag. Fill the cooked egg whites with the mashed yolk mixture. Refrigerate until ready to serve.

For the blue cheese dressing:
In a mixing bowl, whisk together the cheese, buttermilk, mustard, and mayonnaise. Season with salt and pepper as desired.

To assemble and serve:
Fill each egg carton with a combination of deviled eggs and wings: Arrange 3 wings, 2 eggs, and various garnishes in each carton. Fill a clean, intact eggshell half, an egg cup, or a small condiment bowl with some of the blue cheese dressing and set in each carton or beside each carton. You could also pour some of the blue cheese dressing directly into one of the egg spaces in each carton. Serve immediately.

SHRIMP AND GRITS FRIES

Creamy stoneground grits topped with sautéed shrimp is a classic Low Country dish from coastal South Carolina and Georgia. We decided to combine these delicious regional flavors with another American favorite, steak fries (chunky, deep-fried potato fries). Chilled until firm, the shrimp and grits are cut into fry shapes, deep-fried, and served with a white cheddar fondue. It's an interesting bite that is perfect as an appetizer, party snack, or a side dish.

Serves 4

SHRIMP AND GRITS

- **1 pound shrimp (8 to 12 medium shrimp), peeled and deveined**
- **Salt**
- **1 teaspoon black pepper**
- **1 tablespoon unsalted butter**
- **1 tablespoon vegetable oil**
- **2 cups stone-ground white grits**
- **½ cup grated Parmesan cheese**
- **1 tablespoon chopped fresh thyme leaves**
- **1 tablespoon chopped fresh chives**
- **½ cup (1 stick) unsalted butter, cut into ½ pieces**
- **Vegetable oil cooking spray**

For the shrimp and grits:

In a bowl, season the shrimp with 1 teaspoon salt and the pepper and toss to evenly distribute. In a medium skillet over medium-high heat, melt together the butter and oil. Toss in the seasoned shrimp and cook until light brown but opaque in the center, about 1 minute per side. Remove from the heat and allow the shrimp to cool. Chopped the shrimp into small pieces and set aside.

Bring 2 quarts water to a boil in a large saucepan over high heat. Add 1 tablespoon salt and slowly whisk in the grits. Reduce the heat to medium-low and cook, stirring often, until thick and creamy, about 5 to 7 minutes.

Add the diced shrimp, Parmesan cheese, thyme, chives, and butter and stir to combine. Add more salt, if desired.

Spray a rimmed baking sheet (with at least 1-inch high sides) with vegetable oil cooking spray. Spoon in the shrimp and grits and spread out evenly in the pan.

continued

WHITE CHEDDAR FONDUE

- **1 pound white cheddar cheese, shredded**
- **3 tablespoons cornstarch**
- **24 ounces light beer**
- **1 teaspoon freshly grated nutmeg**
- **1 teaspoon dried mustard**
- **Salt**

FRIES

- **6 cups vegetable oil**
- **4 large eggs, beaten**
- **2 cups all-purpose flour**
- **2 cups polenta or fine-ground grits (polenta is a finer grind than grits)**

Spray a sheet of parchment paper trimmed to fit the pan with vegetable oil cooking spray and place the oiled paper on top of the grits. Transfer to the refrigerator to chill until the grits are completely cool.

Once the grits are cooled, invert them onto a cutting board (the parchment that was on top will now be on the bottom) and cut the solid grits into steak-fry shapes. Keep at room temperature until ready to fry or store in the refrigerator for up to 1 hour.

For the fondue:
In a mixing bowl, toss the shredded cheese with the cornstarch to coat the cheese. Set aside.

In a small saucepan set over medium heat, bring the beer to a simmer, being careful not to let it come to a boil. Gradually add the cheese to the beer, a handful at a time, stirring constantly until melted. Remove from the heat and add the nutmeg, dried mustard, and 1 teaspoon salt, stirring to incorporate. Season with salt to taste and keep warm until ready to serve with the fries.

To make the fries:
Heat the oil in a medium saucepan over medium-high heat until it reaches 350°F.

Place the beaten eggs, flour, and polenta in 3 separate bowls. Dredge each grit fry first in the flour (shaking off the excess), then dip into the egg mixture, and finally coat with the dry polenta. Fry the grits fries in the oil until golden brown, about 3 minutes. Remove from the oil and place on a plate or tray lined with paper towels to drain. Serve warm with the white cheddar fondue for dipping.

SAVORY GARDEN POTS

Turn a side table into a potting bench by filling it with these individual salads dressed up as pretty pots of baby spring vegetables. The edible soil is a fanciful way to add rich flavor to the fresh veggies. The baby vegetable crudités are "planted" in the edible soil for guests to pull up and eat. Dipped into or drizzled with the blue cheese dressing, they are a fun way to enjoy a healthy snack or party treat. Create the potting-bench look by stacking up some empty terra-cotta pots. Arrange a couple of the pots on their sides with some of the edible soil spilling out. Embellish the scene with gardening tools and gloves and a small watering can.

Serves 12

SPECIAL EQUIPMENT
- **14 (3-inch) terra-cotta pots**
- **Garden tray or rustic serving tray for holding pots**
- **Decorative garden tools used as props to create your potting-table scene**

EDIBLE SOIL
- **2 cups pitted Kalamata olives, halved**
- **1 pound portobello, shiitake, or button mushrooms, halved**
- **2 to 3 slices toasted pumpernickel bread**
- **¼ cup walnuts, toasted**
- **3 tablespoons brown sugar**
- **1½ teaspoons ground cumin**
- **2 tablespoons cocoa powder**

For the edible soil:
Preheat the oven to 160°F.

Spread the olives on a baking sheet and the mushrooms on another baking sheet and dry in the oven for 8 hours or overnight. Cool completely. Transfer the olives and mushrooms to the bowl of a food processor. Add the toasted walnuts and process until coarsely ground. Transfer to a large bowl and set aside.

Add the toasted bread slices to the food processor and process until fine crumbs form.

Add the bread crumbs to the bowl with the olive mixture. Add the remaining soil ingredients and toss until thoroughly combined. Store in an airtight container for up to 3 weeks.

For the blue cheese dressing:
In a mixing bowl, whisk together all the dressings ingredients. Chill in the refrigerator until ready to use.

- ¼ cup almond flour, toasted
- 2 tablespoons freeze-dried coffee
- Pinch of kosher salt
- 3 pinches of freshly ground black pepper
- ¼ cup black sesame seeds, toasted

BLUE CHEESE DRESSING

- ½ cup crumbled blue cheese
- ⅓ cup buttermilk
- 2 tablespoons Dijon mustard
- 2 tablespoons mayonnaise
- Salt
- Freshly ground black pepper

"PLANTS"

- 3 very small heads baby lettuce
- 12 baby carrots
- 12 baby radishes
- 12 baby cucumbers with flowers
- 12 baby green onions
- ½ cup fresh green peas
- 12 baby corns
- 12 grape tomatoes
- Coriander blossoms
- Pea tendrils
- Variety of edible flowers

To assemble and serve:

Rinse and dry all the crudités. Fill two of the terra-cotta pots with the dressing. Fill each of the remaining pots with some of the edible soil and artfully arrange the "plants" on top, dividing them equally. Arrange the garden pots on a serving tray and place them on your "potting-bench" table to serve. Serve immediately with the blue cheese dressing in the pots on the side for dipping.

YOU CAN NEVER HAVE TOO MUCH

FUN WITH FOOD.

TARTARE PUZZLE

Puzzle-piece shapes are easy to recognize, but are definitely an unexpected shape for serving a steak tartare hors d'oeuvre. Find a puzzle to use as a shape and size guide (we used 5-inch puzzle-piece shapes, which are bite-size) or create your own puzzle-piece shapes.

Serves 6

TARTARE

- **21 ounces best-quality filet mignon**
- **¼ cup ketchup**
- **3 to 4 drops hot sauce, such as Tabasco**
- **¼ cup coarsely chopped capers**
- **2 tablespoons pickle juice**
- **¼ cup chopped red onion**
- **1 tablespoon chopped fresh chives**
- **1 tablespoon white truffle oil**
- **2 tablespoons yellow mustard**
- **12 slices white bread, crusts removed**
- **¼ cup melted butter**

ACCOMPANIMENTS

- **6 hard-boiled eggs, yolks and whites separated**
- **1 tablespoon mayonnaise**
- **Kosher salt**
- **Freshly ground black pepper**
- **¼ cup minced fresh chives**
- **6 caper berries, thinly sliced**
- **½ cup thinly julienned red onion**

For the tartare:
Tightly wrap the filet mignon in plastic wrap and freeze for 2 hours or until mostly firm (this will make it easier to slice). Cut the steak into ¼-inch-thick slices, then finely dice the slices. Transfer to a mixing bowl and add the ketchup, hot sauce, capers, pickle juice, red onion, chives, truffle oil, and mustard. Stir to thoroughly combine, then cover tightly with plastic wrap and refrigerate until ready to serve, up to 1 hour.

Preheat the oven to 325°F.

Roll or press each slice of bread until thin. Using a small sharp knife, cut out one puzzle shape from each piece of bread (making a total of 12), using a 5-inch puzzle-piece shape as a guide. Lightly brush both sides of the bread shapes with some of the melted butter. Arrange the bread pieces on a baking sheet and toast in the oven until light golden brown, about 10 minutes. Set aside to cool completely.

To assemble:
Combine the hard-boiled eggs yolks with the mayonnaise in a food processor and purée until blended. Season with salt and pepper and place in a piping bag.

Grate the egg whites.

Arrange 6 pieces of the toasted bread on a work surface. Pipe the egg yolk mixture around the edges of each piece. Fill in with neat rows of grated egg whites, chives, caper berries, and red onion. Top the remaining 6 pieces of bread with the chilled tartare. Serve each guest a puzzle piece of tartare and a piece with the accompaniments.

ONE-POTATO, TWO-POTATO SALMON

The humble potato gets a luxe makeover when twice baked with buttermilk and crème fraîche and topped with wild salmon fillets. Quickly sautéed broccolini adds a shock of bright green, and tiny marble potatoes—the "two potato" in this dish—are a little surprise, and a reminder that there are hundreds of varieties of potatoes in the world.

Note: *None of these dishes are complicated to make, but the timing is important. Here's a timeline for prepping, cooking, and putting it all together:*

- Bake the Oversized Potatoes.
- While the potatoes are in the oven, blanch the broccolini (see recipe below), make the Chive Cream Sauce, cook the Marble Potatoes and keep warm, then cook the broccolini and keep warm.
- Put the stuffed potatoes in the oven, then cook the salmon.
- Assemble the dish.
- Serve immediately.

Serves 4

MARBLE POTATOES

- **2 tablespoons unsalted butter**
- **1 tablespoon minced shallots**
- **½ teaspoon smoked paprika**
- **½ pound marble (tiny) potatoes, boiled until tender**
- **Sea salt**

In a skillet set over medium heat, melt the butter until frothy. Add the shallots and paprika and sauté until tender. Add the potatoes and continue to cook for 4 to 5 minutes, until warm. Season with salt to taste.

continued

OVERSIZED POTATOES

- **5 huge (about 1½ pounds each) russet potatoes, scrubbed**
- **¼ cup olive oil**
- **3 tablespoons coarse sea salt, divided**
- **1 teaspoon ground cloves, plus extra as needed**
- **½ cup crème fraîche or sour cream**
- **½ cup buttermilk**
- **2 tablespoons unsalted butter, at room temperature**
- **1 tablespoon heavy whipping cream**
- **¼ cup sliced green onions**
- **Freshly grated nutmeg**
- **Ground cloves**
- **⅓ cup minced fresh chives**

Position a rack in the middle of the oven and preheat to 400°F. Pierce each potato in several places with a fork.

In a small mixing bowl, stir together the olive oil, 1 tablespoon of the salt, and ground cloves. Put the potatoes on a baking sheet and rub each potato with some of the seasoned oil to coat completely. Transfer to the oven and bake on the middle rack for 1 to 1½ hours or until cooked through. Remove from the oven and let cool. Reduce the oven temperature to 350°F.

When the potatoes are cool to the touch, slice the top third lengthwise off of four of the potatoes and reserve. Use a spoon to scoop out the insides and transfer to a mixing bowl, leaving about ¼ inch of potato on the skin. Peel the remaining whole potato and cut it into smaller pieces. Transfer the potato pieces to the mixing bowl with the scooped-out potato insides. Add the crème fraiche, buttermilk, butter, cream, and green onions.

Using a large fork or wooden spoon, mash the potatoes together and season with the remaining 2 tablespoons salt, nutmeg, and ground cloves to taste. Spoon the crushed potato mixture back into the 4 potato skins, replace the top third of each potato, and set aside.

When ready to serve, bake the stuffed potatoes for 15 minutes. Sprinkle with minced chives and serve.

CHIVE CREAM SAUCE

Makes 2 cups

- **1 cup shredded Parmesan cheese**
- **1 tablespoon cornstarch**
- **2 cups dry white wine**
- **¼ cup freshly squeezed lemon juice**
- **½ cup chicken stock**
- **½ cup cream cheese**
- **½ tablespoon dry mustard**
- **½ tablespoon freshly grated nutmeg**
- **1 tablespoon salt**
- **2 tablespoons finely chopped fresh chives**

In a mixing bowl, toss together the Parmesan cheese and cornstarch until the cheese is coated. Set aside.

In a medium saucepan, combine the white wine and lemon juice and cook over medium-high heat until reduced by half, about 5 minutes. Add the chicken stock and cook until the liquids are just under a rolling boil. Reduce the heat to medium and slowly stir in the Parmesan cheese until melted and incorporated into the liquid.

Remove from the heat and allow to cool slightly, about 3 minutes. Stir in the cream cheese, dry mustard, nutmeg, salt, and chives until smooth and creamy. Keep warm, stirring occasionally to maintain the creamy texture.

BROCCOLINI

- **1 bunch broccolini**
- **2 tablespoons extra virgin olive oil**
- **1 garlic clove, thinly sliced**
- **¼ teaspoon red pepper flakes**
- **Pinch of smoked paprika**
- **Sea salt**

Fill a large mixing bowl with ice water and set aside.

Fill a medium saucepan about three-quarters full with water and bring to a boil. Add the broccolini and cook until it is bright green and just beginning to turn soft, a few minutes. Remove the broccolini and immediately plunge into the ice water to stop the cooking.

Heat the olive oil in a skillet over medium heat. Add the garlic and sauté until it begins to turn golden. Add the red pepper flakes and paprika and stir until toasted, about 1 to 2 minutes. Add the broccolini and stir until heated through. Season with salt to taste.

WILD SALMON FILLETS

- **4 (7-ounce) wild salmon fillets, such as king salmon or Copper River salmon**
- **2 teaspoons kosher salt**
- **1 teaspoon smoked paprika**
- **1 tablespoon olive oil**

Sprinkle the salmon fillets with the salt and the smoked paprika. Heat the oil in a heavy skillet set over medium-high heat. Cook the salmon for 3 to 4 minutes on each side. Transfer the salmon to a plate.

To assemble the dish:
Place a stuffed potato on each of four individual plates and set the top of each potato to the side. Gently place a salmon fillet on top of each potato and drizzle with Chive Cream Sauce. Arrange the broccolini around each potato and garnish the plates with the marble potatoes. Serve immediately.

ZEN GARDEN

Sophisticated serenity is what this dish evokes. The bed of black rice on the serving plate creates a dramatic backdrop for the glistening, barely cooked tuna. Buy the freshest sushi-grade tuna you can find because the tuna is really the star of the plate. We like to use dark-colored square or rectangular plates for this dish but you can find your zen when you arrange the individual servings and make each plate your own work of art.

Serves 4

- 3 cups granulated sugar
- 1½ cups soy sauce
- ⅔ cup fish sauce
- 1 teaspoon grated lime zest
- ½ cup freshly squeezed lime juice
- ½ cup grated fresh ginger
- 3 tablespoons rice wine vinegar
- 2 teaspoons minced jalapeño
- 1 teaspoon ground coriander seed
- 1 tablespoon chopped fresh cilantro
- 1½ pounds yellowfin (ahi) tuna
- 4 cups freshly cooked and cooled black rice
- ½ cup chopped fresh chives
- 2 tablespoons chopped pickled ginger
- 3 tablespoons simple syrup
- 32 tiny red Baby Bliss potatoes, steamed
- Edible gold spray (available online and at specialty cake decorating stores)
- Yellow pea shoots
- Wasabi peas
- Shredded roasted seaweed (nori)
- Coriander flowers or other herb flowers like basil or chives

Combine the sugar, soy sauce, fish sauce, lime zest and juice, grated fresh ginger, vinegar, and the jalapeño with 1¼ cups water in a medium saucepan. Bring to a boil over high heat. Remove from the heat, add the coriander seed and fresh cilantro, and steep for 1 hour. Refrigerate the marinade to chill completely before using.

Cut the tuna into twenty 1-inch pieces, add to the marinade, and refrigerate for 2 hours.

When ready to serve, stir together the rice, chives, pickled ginger, and simple syrup and set aside.

Spray the tiny potatoes with the gold spray.

To serve, evenly spread 1 cup of rice onto each of four serving dishes. Artfully arrange 5 pieces of tuna on top of the rice and add 8 potatoes to each plate. Garnish each serving with pea shoots, wasabi peas, shredded seaweed, and coriander flowers.

I WAS NEVER
GOOD AT MINDING

MY **MANNERS** AT THE TABLE.

MARSHMALLOW PIZZA

Everyone loves pizza and everyone loves dessert, so why not combine the two? Piped meringue makes the perfect "crust" for these deceptive toppings. Allow your inner molecular gastronomist to emerge by making "onion slices" using agar-agar (available online and at finer groceries and specialty shops), a seaweed-derived gelling agent that allows liquids to solidify at room temperature.

Feel free to follow the recipe below for toppings or come up with your own combinations. It's fun to cut and serve this using a pizza cutter. Add to the scene by placing a block of white chocolate and a cheese grater next to the pizza so that guests can top their slice with extra "cheese" if they like.

Serves 4

SPECIAL EQUIPMENT
- **Piping bag with large round tip**
- **Round cookie cutters in different sizes**
- **Kitchen torch**

MARSHMALLOW CRUST
- **2 tablespoons plus 1½ teaspoons unflavored powdered gelatin**
- **2 cups granulated sugar**
- **2 tablespoons corn syrup**
- **4 large egg whites**
- **Pinch of salt**
- **2 teaspoons vanilla extract**
- **2 to 3 drops of ivory food coloring (available at cake decorating/craft stores)**

For the marshmallow crust:
In a small bowl, sprinkle the gelatin over 2 tablespoons water and set aside to bloom.

Combine the sugar, corn syrup, and ⅔ cup water in a 4-quart saucepan and set over high heat. Stir until the sugar dissolves. Attach a candy thermometer to the saucepan and cook until the mixture reaches 262°F.

Meanwhile, in the bowl of a stand mixer fitted with the whisk attachment, whisk the egg whites on medium speed until frothy. Reduce the speed to low and carefully drizzle in the sugar syrup mixture. Add the gelatin mixture, salt, vanilla extract, and food coloring. Increase the speed to high and whisk until the mixture doubles in volume.

Transfer the marshmallow mixture to a piping bag fitted with large round tip.

continued

strawberry
jelly

marshmallow
crust

white
chocolate

agar
onion rings

AGAR ONION RINGS

- **2 cups coconut milk**
- **1½ teaspoons agar-agar powder (available online or at Whole Foods Market)**
- **¼ cup granulated sugar**

PIZZA TOPPINGS

- **1 cup graham cracker crumbs**
- **¼ cup strawberry jelly**
- **½ cup dark chocolate chips**
- **10 fresh mint leaves, julienned**
- **1½ cups sliced strawberries**
- **Agar Onion Rings (see recipe above)**
- **¼ cup white chocolate chips, melted and placed in a piping bag with a very small tip**
- **Block of white chocolate, for serving (optional)**

On a baking sheet lined with parchment paper, draw a 12-inch circle. Using a spiral motion, pipe the marshmallow mixture inside the circle, starting in the center and working your way to the outline, until the whole surface of the circle is evenly covered. Using a spatula, smooth the surface of the marshmallow "dough." Set aside at room temperature for 15 minutes.

For the agar onion rings:
Line a rimmed baking sheet with plastic wrap. Combine the coconut milk and agar-agar powder in a small saucepan. Set over medium heat and bring just to a boil. Add the sugar and stir until dissolved. Remove from the heat and pour it into the prepared pan. Refrigerate to set and chill. Once solidified, use various-size round cookie cutters to cut it into onion ring shapes: First cut out a larger circle, then use a smaller-diameter cutter to cut out the center of that circle, creating a ring. Use an offset spatula to remove the rings and set them aside on a plate.

To assemble and serve:
Spread the graham cracker crumbs on a baking sheet (to keep the pizza from sticking but also to emulate the semolina flour that pizza makers sprinkle on pizza stones to keep the dough from sticking). Transfer the round of marshmallow dough onto the crumbs. Sprinkle some of the crumbs all around the edges of the dough, creating an outer crust about ½ inch wide.

Spread the strawberry jelly over the surface of the dough, avoiding the outer crust. Sprinkle with dark chocolate chips, julienned mint leaves, and sliced strawberries. Carefully place the agar onion rings on top of the strawberries. Drizzle the melted white chocolate onto the pizza and use a kitchen torch to give the pizza a slightly toasted appearance. Cut into slices and serve with the block of white chocolate and cheese grater alongside for guests to shave onto the pizza, if desired.

CAKE IN PROGRESS

It's the ultimate "If I knew you were coming, I'd have baked a cake" and "Oh, yeah, I already did" moment when guests see eggs, butter, and whipped cream arranged on a cutting board. Watch their faces as they realize that the eggs contain individual, fully baked cakes and the cream and butter (really sticks of buttercream frosting) are the icing for the top.

Note: *You will need a 12-cup muffin pan and 24 clean (blown out—see instructions below) eggshells to make the cakes. You can start cleaning out and collecting eggshells gradually as you use eggs for other recipes. Once clean, the shells can be kept indefinitely.*

Makes 24

EGGSHELL CUPS
- **24 large eggs**

VANILLA CAKE
- **¾ cup whole milk**
- **8 large egg whites, lightly beaten**
- **1½ teaspoons vanilla extract**
- **2 cups cake flour**
- **1 tablespoon baking powder**
- **1 teaspoon salt**
- **½ cup (1 stick) unsalted butter, at room temperature**
- **1⅛ cups granulated sugar**

For the eggshell cups:
Wash and dry the eggs. Gently insert a long needle into the large end of the egg to make a small hole. Twist the needle as you push it into the eggshell as far as you can. Use the same needle to make a slightly larger hole in the small end of the egg. Push the needle into the center of the egg and move it around to break the yolk. Hold the egg over a bowl with the small end down. Blow firmly into the large end of the egg until all of the egg yolk and white comes out of the hole in the small end. Rinse out the egg by running a thin stream of water into the larger hole. Blow out the excess water. Stand the eggs, large end facing down, in a dish drainer to dry completely.

For the cake:
Preheat the oven to 325°F. Line each cup of a 12-cup muffin tin with aluminum foil so that an egg will stand upright in each cup. Place one cleaned egg in each cup.

In a medium mixing bowl, stir together the milk, egg whites, and vanilla and set aside. In a separate bowl, whisk together the flour, baking powder, and salt.

continued

whipped
cream

strawberry
topping

vanilla
cake

buttercream
frosting

BUTTERCREAM FROSTING

- **½ cup (1 stick) unsalted butter, at room temperature**
- **1 teaspoon vanilla extract**
- **½ teaspoon salt**
- **1 cup confectioners' sugar**
- **1 tablespoon milk**
- **1 to 2 drops yellow food coloring**

WHIPPED CREAM

- **2 cups heavy whipping cream**
- **2 tablespoons granulated sugar**
- **1 teaspoon vanilla extract**

FRUIT TOPPING

- **Fresh fruit or fruit compote (optional)**

In the bowl of a stand mixer fitted with the paddle attachment, beat the butter for 30 seconds. With the mixer on low, gradually add the sugar. Increase the speed to medium and beat for 2 minutes or until light and fluffy, stopping to scrape down the sides of the bowl once or twice. With the mixer on low speed, add one-third of the flour mixture, then one-third of the milk mixture, beating to incorporate after each addition. Continue alternating dry and wet ingredients until all are incorporated, stopping to scrape down the sides of the bowl as needed.

Transfer the cake batter from the mixing bowl into a pitcher or large measuring cup with a pouring spout. Carefully pour the batter into empty eggshells, filling them only halfway. You can also do this by filling a disposable pastry bag with the cake batter and cutting a small hole in the tip, then filling the eggs by squeezing the batter carefully into the egg through the hole. Fill all of the eggs halfway and bake for 8 to 10 minutes. You will be able to see the spongy cake through the hole. Insert a toothpick or a wooden skewer into one of the holes in the egg and pull out to test for doneness. If the toothpick is clean (not coated with batter), the cakes are done. Let the eggshell cakes cool completely in the pan.

For the buttercream:
Line a small baking sheet or small glass baking dish with plastic wrap.

In the bowl of a stand mixer fitted with the paddle attachment, beat the butter, vanilla, and salt on medium speed until well blended. Gradually add the confectioners' sugar and mix on low speed until just combined.

Increase the speed to medium, add the milk and food coloring, and beat until creamy and free of lumps.

Transfer the buttercream to the prepared baking dish, spreading it into a 1-inch-thick, even layer. Place in the freezer for 1 hour or until frozen. Cut the frozen buttercream into blocks resembling sticks of butter and return to the refrigerator until ready to serve.

For the whipped cream:
Prepare just before serving.

Whisk the heavy cream, sugar, and vanilla extract in a large, metal mixing bowl until medium peaks form.

Transfer to a decorative mixing bowl and serve immediately. (The whipped cream will stay fresh for about 1 hour at room temperature.)

To serve:
Prepare a kitchen cutting board or large tray to look like you are getting ready to bake a cake. Place the egg cakes in a decorative mixing bowl or a basket filled with straw or grass with one or two of the eggs cracked halfway to reveal the cake inside. Place the peeled-away shells in another decorative bowl placed on the tray or board so that your guests will know what to do with the shells once they crack their own egg cakes open. Place the bar of buttercream on a small butter dish or plate with a butter knife next to it. You should cut 1 or 2 "pats of butter" away from the bar so that guests will know to cut into the buttercream bar and spread the frosting onto their eggs.

In another bowl on the tray, display the whipped cream and put a mixing spoon or spatula into the cream so that guests will know to put a little on their egg cake. You can also crumble any extra cake into another mixing bowl, put a few buttercream "butter pats" on top of the crumbles, and place a rubber spatula or spoon in the bowl to make it look like flour and sugar ready to be mixed together. Guests can scoop out some of the cake crumbles with a pat of buttercream and perhaps top with some fresh fruit as an additional flavor element.

SWEET GARDEN POTS

Returning to the garden for inspiration, we have taken tiny garden pots and turned them into free-form cupcakes. Filled with crumbled brownies for soil and "green velvet" cake for moss, the pots are "planted" with delicious fruits and fillings to make individual desserts. This is another creation where garden props can be a fantastic addition to your serving scenario. Find small garden signs or use wooden craft sticks to label the fruit-and-filling combinations in each pot.

Serves 12

SPECIAL EQUIPMENT
- **12 (3-inch) terra-cotta pots, cleaned well**
- **Garden tags or mini plant markers and decorative garden tools for propping the scene**
- **Garden tray, for serving**

EMERALD SPONGE CAKE (page 167)

BROWNIE SOIL (page 168)

"PLANTS"
- **1 cup peanut butter, divided**
- **2 bananas, peeled and sliced**
- **1 pint strawberries, 4 left whole for garnish and the remaining sliced**
- **1 cup freshly whipped cream**
- **2 bunches fresh mint**
- **Baby spinach, lettuce, or other green edible leaves**

Crumble the emerald sponge cake and brownie soil into two separate bowls.

Assemble the desserts by adding some of the brownie soil to each pot, dividing equally.

Add ¼ cup peanut butter to four of the pots and top with the sliced bananas, dividing equally. Add the sliced strawberries to another four of the pots, dividing equally, and top with a dollop of whipped cream. Add some whipped cream and a few fresh mint leaves to the four remaining pots.

Top each pot with some more of the brownie crumbles and add some of the crumbled emerald sponge cake to each pot to look like moss.

Garnish the mint pots with some additional mint leaves. Garnish the strawberry pots each with a whole strawberry. Garnish the peanut butter pots with some green edible leaves. Place the pots on a tray with decorative garden tools and serve.

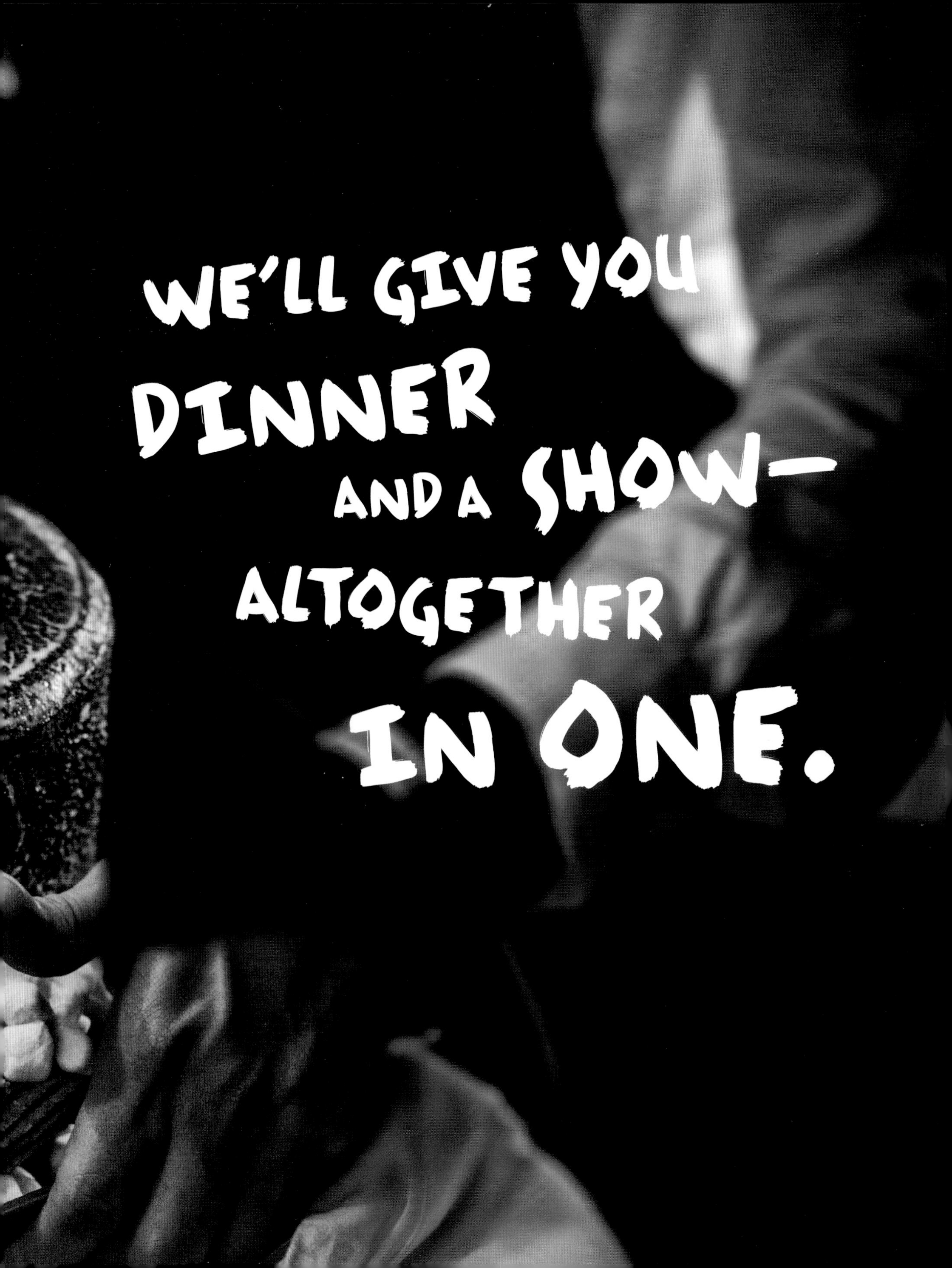

WE'LL GIVE YOU
DINNER
AND A SHOW—
ALTOGETHER
IN ONE.

sponge
cakes

blue
Curaçao

whipped
cream

phyllo
scrubbies

SPONGES

AND SCRUBBIES

When dinner is over and all the plates are cleared, announce to your guests that it's time to do the dishes. They won't consider it a chore when they discover that the stack of dirty dishes and kitchen sponges is actually an array of tender angel food cakes, phyllo-dough pastries, freshly whipped cream, and strawberry sauce.

You can make this pop-art dessert look more like a dirty dish pile by stacking up dishes smeared with chocolate bars and grated chocolate, fruit preserves, and sweet sauces (see recipes on page 94). Allow the shapes and colors of your real kitchen sponges to be your guide when cutting out the sponge shapes.

Note: You will need two or three 9 x 5 x 3-inch loaf pans to bake this angel food–style cake.

Makes 8 to 10 "sponges" and 4 to 6 "scrubbies"

SPONGE CAKES

- **2 cups cake flour**
- **3 cups granulated sugar**
- **24 large egg whites**
- **2 tablespoons warm water**
- **1 teaspoon table salt**
- **1 teaspoon cream of tartar**
- **1 teaspoon vanilla extract**
- **Food coloring in 3 or 4 different colors**

Preheat the oven to 350°F.

In a mixing bowl, sift together the cake flour and sugar and set aside.

In the bowl of a stand mixer fitted with the whisk attachment, beat together the egg whites and warm water on high speed until soft peaks begin to form. Add the salt, cream of tartar, and vanilla and mix until incorporated into the soft peaks, about 1 minute. Reduce the speed to low and gradually add the flour-sugar mixture, mixing only until incorporated.

continued

Divide the batter among 3 or 4 separate bowls (you can keep some in the mixer bowl) and add a small amount of a different food coloring to each batch to create different batter colors. Pour one color of cake batter into a pan in about a 1-inch-thick layer, then top with a different color. This process will make the cakes look like multicolored kitchen sponges. You can also bake the cakes in a single color, if desired. Just be sure to fill up the loaf pans about halfway up no matter how many colors you use for each cake. (This is an angel food–style cake, so greasing is not necessary—grease will cause the cake to cook very flat.) Bake the cakes for about 20 minutes, until golden on top and springy to the touch.

Allow the cakes to cool completely in the pans before turning out onto a flat surface or cutting board. You can use a small sharp knife to run between the cake and the sides of the pan before inverting to facilitate unmolding. Gently trim the cake into kitchen sponge shapes using an electric knife or serrated knife.

METHOD TO THE MADNESS: *"Sponge" Cakes*

PHYLLO SCRUBBIES

SPECIAL EQUIPMENT
- Edible silver dust (available online and in cake decorating supply stores)
- 12-cup muffin pan

- ½ pound (half of a 16-ounce package) frozen shredded phyllo dough (also known as *kataifi*), thawed
- ½ cup (1 stick) unsalted butter, melted
- ¼ cup granulated sugar, divided
- 3 tablespoons edible silver dust
- 1½ tablespoon vodka or flavored liqueur (such as Grand Marnier or Amaretto)

Note: *The liqueur is used as a medium for the silver dust to be mixed with so that it will adhere to the pastry. Liqueur works best for this because it has a high alcohol content and evaporates quickly, which keeps the silver dust and the surface you are painting it on from becoming gummy.)*

Preheat the oven to 350°F and grease 4 to 6 cups in a 12-cup muffin pan.

Stretch out the phyllo dough and separate it into 6-inch-long bunches. Place the bunches on a work surface and brush each bunch with some of the melted butter. Sprinkle the bunches with 2 tablespoons of the sugar. Create a "scrubby" shape by forming each bunch into a ball. Place each "scrubby" bunch into a greased muffin cup. Brush the tops with the remaining melted butter and sprinkle with the remaining 2 tablespoons sugar.

Bake until golden brown and crisp around the edges, 15 to 20 minutes. Allow the "scrubbies" to cool before gently removing them from the muffin pan.

In a small bowl, mix together the silver dust and the liqueur. Using a small paintbrush or pastry brush, gently dab the silver mixture all over the crispy dough to paint it silver like a scouring pad.

METHOD TO THE MADNESS: *Phyllo "Scrubbies"*

STRAWBERRY SAUCE

Makes 1¼ cups

- **1 cup chopped fresh strawberries**
- **¼ cup granulated sugar**
- **1 tablespoon freshly squeezed lemon juice**

Combine the strawberries, sugar, and lemon juice in a medium saucepan over medium-low heat. Cook, stirring occasionally, for about 7 minutes, until the strawberries become soft. Transfer to a blender and purée the strawberry mixture until smooth. Store, covered, in the refrigerator for up to 2 days until ready to serve.

BLUE CURAÇAO "DISH DETERGENT"

Makes ¾ cup

- **¼ cup granulated sugar**
- **2 tablespoons blue curaçao liqueur**

Combine the sugar, liqueur, and ¼ cup water in a small saucepan over medium-high heat. Bring the ingredients to a boil, stirring occasionally. Remove from the heat and allow to cool. Transfer to a clean squeeze bottle, glass cruet, or other container that looks like a dish detergent bottle and refrigerate until serving.

WHIPPED CREAM "SOAPSUDS"

Makes 1½ cups

- **1 cup heavy whipping cream**
- **1 tablespoon granulated sugar**
- **1 teaspoon vanilla extract**
- **6 tablespoons chocolate syrup**

In the bowl of a stand mixer fitted with the whisk attachment, whip the heavy cream on high until soft peaks begin to form. Add the sugar and vanilla and continue mixing for another minute or two until the whipped cream looks like billowy soapsuds.

For the assembly:

Stack as many dishes as you like onto a tray or in a clean, plastic "dish tub." Arrange the sponge cakes and scrubby pads around and on top of the plates. Smear the plates and sponges with the strawberry sauce, and drizzle with the blue curaçao "dish detergent." Smear the chocolate syrup over the dishes and dollop with whipped cream "soapsuds" to create a sink full of dirty dishes.

DESSERT CAMP

A build-your-own bananas Foster and cherries jubilee dessert bar gets served up camp-style, with "tin" cans used as serving bowls for homemade vanilla ice cream and warm caramel sauce. You can "set up camp" by covering a table with a camping blanket or a quilt and arranging vintage camping equipment as center-pieces. Canteens from old scouting days or new ones purchased at camping supply sections are also great receptacles for the caramel sauce. Decorate the table with pinecones and use scouting utensils. Then sing campfire songs and tell ghost stories when you are full.

Note: Use cleaned food cans (from tomatoes, beans, soup, or coffee) as holders for the ice cream or sauces here. New "sardine" type cans are available online or at the Container Store. (You can also save and wash actual sardine cans in your dishwasher if you eat a lot of sardines!) The desserts in our camp are baked in the sardine cans.

Serves 4 to 6

VANILLA ICE CREAM

- **1 cup whole milk**
- **¾ cup granulated sugar**
- **2 cups heavy whipping cream, divided**
- **Pinch of salt**
- **1 vanilla bean, split in half lengthwise**
- **6 large egg yolks, beaten**
- **¾ teaspoon vanilla extract**

CARAMEL SAUCE

- **¾ cup (1½ sticks) unsalted butter**
- **1½ cups firmly packed light brown sugar**
- **¼ teaspoon salt**
- **¾ cup evaporated milk**
- **1 tablespoon vanilla extract**

For the vanilla ice cream:

Combine the milk, sugar, 1 cup of the heavy cream, and the salt in a medium saucepan over low heat and stir until the sugar is dissolved. Scrape the seeds from the vanilla bean into the milk mixture, then add the beanpod. Remove from the heat, cover, and let the milk mixture steep at room temperature for 30 minutes.

Pour the remaining 1 cup heavy cream into a mixing bowl and set a fine-mesh sieve on top of the bowl. Place the beaten egg yolks in a separate bowl and slowly pour the warm milk mixture into the eggs, whisking constantly. Return the mixture to the saucepan. Place the saucepan over medium heat and stir constantly with a rubber spatula until the mixture thickens, coats the back of the spatula, and reaches 170° to 175°F.

Pour the custard through the fine-mesh sieve into the bowl of heavy cream. Add the vanilla bean to the bowl, stir in the vanilla extract, and place the bowl over an ice bath. Stir until the mixture is cool to the touch. Cover and refrigerate at least 8 hours or overnight.

continued

vanilla ice cream

bananas foster

cherries jubilee

CHERRIES JUBILEE

- **¼ cup granulated sugar**
- **2 tablespoons cornstarch**
- **¼ cup cherry juice**
- **¼ cup orange juice**
- **1 pound frozen pitted cherries**
- **¼ teaspoon kirsch liqueur**
- **¼ cup brandy**

BANANAS FOSTER

- **4 tablespoons (½ stick) unsalted butter**
- **½ cup (firmly packed) dark brown sugar**
- **3½ tablespoons dark rum**
- **1½ teaspoons vanilla extract**
- **½ teaspoon ground cinnamon**
- **3 bananas, peeled and halved lengthwise**

When ready to churn the ice cream, remove the vanilla bean, transfer the mixture to an ice cream maker and process according to the manufacturer's instructions. Transfer to the freezer until ready to serve.

For the caramel sauce:
In a medium saucepan, combine the butter, brown sugar, salt, and 2 tablespoons water. Set over medium heat and bring to a boil, stirring constantly. Boil for 3 to 5 minutes, or until the mixture has thickened and is the consistency of a pourable sauce. Remove from the heat and slowly whisk in the evaporated milk and vanilla extract. Let cool to room temperature.

For the cherries jubilee:
Whisk the sugar and cornstarch together in a medium saucepan. Add the cherry juice and orange juice and whisk until well combined. Set over medium-high heat and bring to a boil, whisking until thickened. Add the cherries, stir, and return to a boil. Reduce the heat to low and simmer for 10 minutes. Remove from the heat and stir in the kirsch. Add the brandy and ignite using a long lighter. Gently shake the pan until the flame extinguishes.

For the bananas Foster:
In a large skillet set over medium heat, melt the butter. Add the sugar, rum, and vanilla extract. Stir to combine and cook until the mixture bubbles. Add the bananas to the pan, cut-side down, and cook until they caramelize, 2 to 3 minutes. Flip the bananas and cook for another 2 to 3 minutes.

YOU CAN PLAY WITH YOUR FOOD

SEEDLING SALAD

Baby vegetables are so beautiful and concentrated with flavor. I love using them for dynamic hors d'oeuvres. Gardens supply constant inspiration for me and this arrangement is another way to feature my "edible soil" as the base for healthy party food. It's fun to collect colorful seed packets and use garden tools, twine, and other garden implements as props in your garden scene.

Serves 4

SPECIAL EQUIPMENT
- **4 empty garden-seed packets**

BABY CRUDITÉS
- **3 heads baby lettuce**
- **8 baby carrots**
- **8 baby radishes**
- **8 baby green onions**
- **8 baby beets**
- **8 baby cauliflower florets**
- **4 baby green onions**
- **¼ cup fresh green peas**
- **12 grape tomatoes**

- **Edible Soil (page 64)**
- **4 coriander blossoms**
- **Variety of edible flowers**

Rinse and dry all the crudités. Fill each seed packet with some of the edible soil and spread the remaining soil on a large serving platter. Artfully arrange a variety of baby crudités on and around the soil as well as in the tops of the seed packets. Nestle the seed packets among the crudités on the platter. Garnish with the coriander blossoms and edible flowers. Serve immediately.

THYME CHICKS
WITH CHERRY AND CRANBERRY MARMALADE

Perfect for a springtime brunch or garden party, these savory scones are shaped like little chicks. Baked until golden and served in a wheatgrass-lined basket or wooden crate, these are delicious topped with creamy butter and my sweet-tart marmalade.

Makes 2 dozen chicks

SPECIAL EQUIPMENT
- **Pastry bag with a large round tip**
- **Decorative basket or crate**
- **Fresh wheatgrass (available at some grocery stores or health food markets)**

CHERRY AND CRANBERRY MARMALADE
- **1½ cups pitted fresh cherries**
- **1 cup dried cranberries**
- **½ cup granulated sugar**
- **¼ cup red wine vinegar**
- **3 tablespoons cranberry juice**
- **2 tablespoons cornstarch**

For the marmalade:

Combine the cherries, cranberries, sugar, vinegar, and 1 cup water in a medium saucepan over medium heat. Cook, stirring frequently, for 30 minutes, or until the mixture has thickened and darkened in color.

Whisk together the cranberry juice and cornstarch in a small bowl until there are no lumps. Add the slurry to the fruit mixture in the pan and bring just to a boil. Remove from the heat. Transfer the mixture to the bowl of a food processor and pulse 8 to 10 times. Return the mixture to the saucepan and cool completely in the pan before refrigerating in an airtight container until ready to use.

For the chicks:

Preheat the oven to 425°F. In a small saucepan set over medium-high heat, add 1 cup of water to the butter, sugar, and salt. Bring to a boil. Add the flour and the thyme and remove from the heat. Using a rubber heat-resistant spatula, stir the flour into the mixture and then return to the heat, stirring continuously until the dough forms a ball. Transfer the ball to the bowl of an electric mixer fitted with a paddle attachment, and allow the dough to cool for about 5 minutes. With the mixer on low speed, add the eggs—including the 2 extra egg whites, one at a time, incorporating each egg before adding the next. Mix just until the mixture is smooth, about 1 minute. Place the dough into a large piping bag fitted with a large round tip.

continued

CHICKS

- **6 tablespoons unsalted butter**
- **½ teaspoon sugar**
- **1 teaspoon salt**
- **¾ cup all-purpose flour**
- **2 teaspoons chopped fresh thyme leaves**
- **4 large eggs plus 2 egg whites**
- **1 teaspoon black sesame seeds**

DECORATIONS

- **2 tablespoons unsalted butter, melted**
- **2 cups graham cracker crumbs**

- **Cherry and Cranberry Marmalade (page 103), for serving**

Line a sheet tray with a silicone mat or parchment paper. To form the chicks, touch the tip of the bag to the sheet tray and hold the bag almost parallel to the sheet. Begin to pipe out one ball that is about 1 ½ inches in diameter, and as you finish squeezing, drag the bag away from the ball to create the tail of the chick. The shape will be sort of a sideways teardrop. This will be the bottom part of the chick. Next, pipe a slightly smaller ball on top of the fattest part of the teardrop shape and with your pastry bag at a 45-degree angle, quickly lift the bag away to create a little pointed beak shape. You can use slightly wet fingers to manipulate the shape a bit if you like. Stick the sesame seeds on the sides of the chicks' heads to create eyes.

Cook the chicks for 10 minutes at 425°F, then turn the oven temperature down to 350°F and bake for 10 more minutes or until brown. Remove from the oven and immediately pierce the main body of the chicks slightly with a paring knife to allow the steam to escape. Allow to cool for just a few minutes and then remove from the tray, transferring the chicks, upright, to a cool baking sheet tray or cooling racks. These are best eaten within a couple of hours of baking.

To decorate the chicks:
Lightly brush the chicks on all sides with the melted butter and roll in the graham cracker crumbs. Serve with the marmalade.

SAVORY ANIMAL CRACKERS

Cheese crackers take on a nostalgic form when cut into animal cracker shapes. Who says animal crackers have to be sweet or that they are just for kids? It's so much fun to present these spilling out of colorful boxes at a cocktail party.

Makes approximately 30 crackers

- **1 pound sharp cheddar cheese, shredded**
- **1 cup (2 sticks) unsalted butter, at room temperature**
- **1½ cups bread flour, plus extra for rolling**
- **½ teaspoon table salt**
- **¼ teaspoon ground white pepper**
- **¼ teaspoon cayenne pepper**

Combine the cheese and butter in the bowl of a stand mixer fitted with the paddle attachment. Beat on low speed for 1 to 2 minutes just to combine. Add the flour, salt, white pepper, and cayenne pepper and beat on medium speed for 3 to 4 minutes until all the ingredients are incorporated and a ball of dough is formed. Shape the dough into a disc, wrap in plastic wrap, and refrigerate for 30 minutes.

Line 2 rimmed baking sheets with parchment paper. Remove the dough from the refrigerator and roll out to ¼-inch thickness on a lightly floured surface.

Using 2-inch animal-shaped cookie cutters, cut out crackers and arrange them ½ inch apart on the prepared baking sheets. Gather the dough scraps together and roll them out again, until all the dough has been used. Return the dough to the refrigerator if it becomes too soft to easily roll. Refrigerate the crackers in the refrigerator for 30 minutes.

Preheat the oven to 300°F.

Bake the crackers for 15 minutes or until they are lightly browned and cooked through. Remove from the oven and allow to cool on the pan for about 5 minutes before gently moving them to a metal cooling rack. Cool completely and store in an airtight container until ready to serve.

EVERYTHING TASTES BETTER WHEN YOU EAT IT WITH YOUR HANDS.

ROLL YOUR OWN
SHRIMP AND VEGETABLES

I've always loved the way fresh spring rolls look—so light and transparent—almost like looking through a kaleidoscope. The technique for this recipe came from that inspiration, and because the rice paper is laid out flat, the fillings can be arranged in a pattern. The rolls can be assembled ahead of time or the ingredients can be set out and guests encouraged to arrange the fillings to their liking and then "roll their own" for dipping into sauce and eating.

Serves 4

SHRIMP AND MARINADE
- **1½ cups granulated sugar**
- **¼ cup soy sauce**
- **1 stalk lemongrass, chopped**
- **1 tablespoon sliced peeled fresh ginger**
- **1 teaspoon red pepper flakes**
- **Zest and juice of 1 lime**
- **2 teaspoons fish sauce**
- **2 tablespoons grenadine**
- **3 sprigs fresh cilantro**
- **1 pound large shrimp, peeled and deveined**
- **1 tablespoon cornstarch**

SUMMER ROLLS
- **8 sheets round rice paper**
- **4 sprigs fresh cilantro, picked into small pieces**
- **2 sprigs fresh basil, picked into small pieces**

For the shrimp and marinade:
Combine 1 cup water with the sugar, soy sauce, lemongrass, ginger, red pepper flakes, lime zest and juice, fish sauce, and grenadine in a small saucepan. Bring to a boil over high heat. Remove from the heat, add the cilantro sprigs, and cover and steep for 45 minutes. Strain through a sieve into a bowl and discard the solids. Transfer the marinade to the refrigerator to cool completely.

Reserve ½ cup of the marinade. Place the shrimp in the bowl with the remaining marinade. Cover and refrigerate for 4 hours.

Preheat the oven to 350°F. Line a rimmed baking sheet with parchment paper.

Drain the shrimp, discard the marinade in the bowl, and arrange the shrimp on the prepared baking sheet (the shrimp should not be touching). Bake for 10 minutes, or until cooked through. Transfer the cooked shrimp to the refrigerator to chill completely.

continued

- **4 fresh chives, picked into small pieces**
- **½ cucumber, sliced into thin strips**
- **1 medium carrot, peeled and sliced into thin strips**
- **¼ cup thinly sliced strips red pepper**
- **2 candied kumquats, thinly sliced**
- **1 radish, sliced into thin rounds**
- **2 canned hearts of palm, sliced into thin rings**
- **2 tablespoons black sesame seeds**

Place the reserved ½ cup marinade in a small saucepan and bring to a boil. Whisk the cornstarch with 1 tablespoon water in a small bowl to create a slurry. Add the slurry to the marinade and whisk until it has the consistency of a smooth sauce. Set aside at room temperature.

To assemble and serve the summer rolls:
Fill a large bowl halfway with cold water. Place one sheet of rice paper in the bowl of water and let sit until soft and pliable. Remove the rice paper from the water, letting the excess drain off. Place the rice paper down on a work surface and sprinkle some of the fresh herbs over the top. Next, arrange the slices of carrot, cucumber, and pepper on top.

Then, creatively arrange some of the shrimp, kumquats, radish, sesame seeds, and hearts of palm. Roll up tightly. (You can cut the roll into smaller pieces, if you like.) Serve with the marinade sauce, and garnish with more fresh herbs and sesame seeds. Repeat with remaining ingredients to make a total of 4 rolls. Serve immediately.

BUCKET OF BONES

WITH CREAMY CUCUMBER CHUTNEY

I love to have some fun when dreaming up recipe names and presentations. Everyone loves messy finger food like ribs and wings, and their shapes allow us to make playful piles or sculptures on a tray. In this case, a bucket for serving the "bones" invites diners to feel free to get their hands dirty and dig in. At the restaurant, we like to put some smoldering wood chips and herbs on the serving platter to really make the experience of being at a true barbecue come to life.

Serves 4

BBQ DRY RUB

- **1 cup firmly packed brown sugar**
- **2 tablespoons instant coffee**
- **2 tablespoons chili powder**
- **1 tablespoon onion powder**
- **½ tablespoon freshly ground black pepper**
- **1 teaspoon ground white pepper**

CREAMY CUCUMBER CHUTNEY

- **2 large cucumbers, seeded and diced**
- **2 garlic cloves, minced**
- **2 tablespoons chopped fresh dill**
- **½ cup Major Grey's chutney**
- **¼ cup sour cream**
- **¼ cup Greek-style yogurt**
- **Juice of 1 lemon**
- **½ teaspoon ground cinnamon**
- **½ teaspoon ground cumin**

For the BBQ dry rub:
Place all the ingredients in a mixing bowl and stir to combine. Set aside until ready to use.

For the cucumber chutney:
Place all the ingredients in a mixing bowl and stir to combine. Cover and refrigerate until ready to use.

For the bourbon BBQ sauce:
Melt the butter in a large saucepan over medium heat. Add the onions, garlic, ginger, fennel, coriander, and cumin and cook until the onions are translucent, about 5 minutes.

Reduce the heat to low and add the balsamic vinegar and pineapple juice. Cook until reduced to a light syrup that coats the back of a spoon, approximately 7 minutes.

Add the remaining ingredients except the bourbon; simmer over low heat for 30 minutes, stirring frequently. Add the bourbon and cook for an additional 10 minutes.

continued

BOURBON BBQ SAUCE

- ½ cup (1 stick) unsalted butter
- 2 onions, finely chopped
- 3 garlic cloves, crushed
- 1 tablespoon minced peeled fresh ginger
- 2 tablespoons fennel seed
- 1 tablespoon coriander seed
- 1 tablespoon cumin seed
- 6 tablespoons balsamic vinegar
- 1 cup pineapple juice
- 1 (32-ounce) bottle ketchup
- 2 tablespoons Worcestershire sauce
- 1 tablespoon honey
- 2 tablespoons soy sauce
- 2 tablespoons sweet soy sauce
- 1 cup firmly packed brown sugar
- 1 teaspoon dry mustard
- 1 cinnamon stick
- 4 bay leaves
- 3 large sprigs fresh basil, leaves coarsely chopped
- 1 cup bourbon

"BONES"

- 1 rack baby back ribs, cut into 2 bone sections
- 8 ounces or 4 pieces Korean-style beef short ribs
- 1 cup bourbon
- 12 chicken wings
- 1 rack of lamb, cut into 8 pieces
- 1 pound apple wood chips, soaked in water
- 2 cinnamon sticks, soaked in water
- 8 fresh rosemary branches

Remove the pan from the heat and allow the sauce to cool slightly in the pan. Using an immersion blender, purée the sauce in the pan until smooth. Pour through a fine-mesh strainer into a bowl and cool completely before using.

For the "bones":
Evenly spread the baby back and short ribs on a large baking sheet, season on all sides with the BBQ dry rub, and refrigerate for 24 hours.

Preheat the oven to 300°F. Place a metal cooling rack in a large roasting pan. Pour 1 cup of bourbon in the bottom of the pan and then add enough water to come just beneath but not touching the rack (this will create steam to cook the ribs in moist heat). Evenly spread the ribs on the rack, cover tightly with foil, and bake for 2½ hours or until tender. Reserve until ready to finish on the grill.

Heat a grill to medium-low heat. Place half of the wood chips in an aluminum foil pan or pouch and set on one side of the grill to create smoke. Season the chicken wings and lamb chops on all sides with salt and the BBQ dry rub. Place the wings on the grill and cook, flipping the wings every 10 minutes until cooked through, approximately 30 minutes.

Increase the heat on the grill to medium and then add the remaining wood chips, the cinnamon sticks, and rosemary branches to the foil pan. Place the lamb chops, baby back ribs and short ribs on the grill and cook for 10 to 15 minutes, flipping halfway through. Return the wings to the grill and reduce the heat to low. Brush everything with the bourbon BBQ sauce, close the lid, cook for 10 minutes, then add another coating of sauce. Repeat one more time until each set of bones has a baked-on glaze coating.

Serve hot with the cucumber chutney alongside.

COOKIE PAINTBRUSHES

While artfully presented dishes are specialties of the house, this one encourages you to pick up a "brush" and coat it with edible "paint." To make the presentation look even more artistic, you can arrange the paintbrush-shaped cookies and bowls of the colored white chocolate ganache for dipping on an actual artist's palette instead of a serving tray.

Note: *The colored chocolate "paint" is made using white chocolate pistoles. Pistoles are button-shaped pastry-grade (couverture) chocolates that create an especially smooth, shiny texture when melted together with heavy cream. It's important to use oil-based food coloring when adding tint to chocolate because liquid coloring would cause the chocolate to seize and a powder would not distribute evenly. Chocolate pistoles and oil-based food colorings are available online and in specialty stores.*

Makes about 4 dozen cookies

SUGAR COOKIE BRUSHES
- **2 cups (4 sticks) unsalted butter, at room temperature**
- **1 cup granulated sugar**
- **2 cups all-purpose flour, plus additional for dusting**
- **¼ teaspoon table salt**
- **½ cup mini chocolate chips**
- **½ cup semisweet chocolate chunks**
- **½ cup macadamia nuts, toasted**

For the sugar cookie brushes:
Preheat the oven to 325°F. Line a baking sheet with parchment paper. In the bowl of a stand mixer fitted with the paddle attachment, beat the butter and sugar on medium-high speed until creamy. Reduce the speed to low and gradually add the flour and salt until combined.

Divide the dough among three small bowls. In the first bowl, fold in the mini chocolate chips. In the second bowl, fold in the semisweet chocolate chunks. In the third bowl, fold in the toasted macadamia nuts.

Lightly flour a work surface. Working with each dough mixture separately, pinch off golf-ball-size pieces. Using your hands, roll each of the balls into a log shape. Using a rolling pin, roll each log into a ½-inch-thick strip. Each of the strips can be a different size—these will be your cookie "paintbrushes" and will look more authentic if they are not all exactly the same.

Place the strips on the prepared baking sheet. Bake until golden brown, 8 to 12 minutes. Allow the cookie brushes to cool completely. Leave the oven on for the chocolate brushes.

continued

CHOCOLATE BRUSHES

- **2 cups (4 sticks) unsalted butter, at room temperature**
- **1 cup granulated sugar**
- **2 cups all-purpose flour, plus additional for dusting**
- **1 cup unsweetened cocoa powder**
- **½ teaspoon table salt**
- **½ cup mini chocolate chips**
- **½ cup white chocolate chunks**
- **½ cup coarsely chopped dry-roasted peanuts**

COLORED GANACHE

- **1 tablespoon seedless raspberry jelly**
- **1 tablespoon dried food-grade lavender (lavender flower buds)**
- **1 teaspoon orange zest**
- **½ teaspoon lime zest**
- **4 cups heavy whipping cream**
- **1 pound (about 2 cups) white chocolate pistoles**
- **1 tablespoon oil-based food coloring in 4 different colors: red, blue, yellow, and green**

For the chocolate brushes:

Preheat the oven to 325°F. Line a baking sheet with parchment paper.

In the bowl of a stand mixer fitted with the paddle attachment, beat the butter and sugar on medium-high speed until creamy. In a separate bowl, combine the flour, cocoa, and salt. Turn the mixer to low speed and gradually add the flour mixture until combined. Divide the dough among three small bowls. In the first bowl, fold in the mini chocolate chips. In the second bowl, fold in the white chocolate chunks. In the third bowl, fold in the peanuts.

Lightly flour a work surface. Working with each dough mixture separately, pinch off golf-ball-size pieces. Using your hands, roll each piece into a log shape. Using a rolling pin, roll each log into a ½-inch-thick strip. Each of the strips can be a different size—these will be cookie "paintbrushes" and will look more authentic if they are not all exactly the same. Place the strips on the prepared baking sheet. Bake until firm, about 8 to 12 minutes. Allow the cookie brushes to cool completely.

For the ganache:

Place the raspberry jelly, dried lavender, orange zest, and lime zest in four separate small bowls.

In a small saucepan, bring the cream just to a simmer and remove from the heat. Slowly divide the hot cream among the bowls (1 cup cream per bowl). Add 3 drops of red food coloring to the bowl with the raspberry jelly, 3 drops of blue food coloring to the bowl with the lavender, 3 drops of yellow food coloring to the bowl with the orange zest, and 3 drops of green food coloring to the bowl with the lime zest. Let these mixtures steep for approximately 10 minutes.

Once the cream in each bowl has cooled, strain each bowl separately into four separate, clean containers. Keeping each mixture separate, reheat in a small saucepan until simmering. Return the heated, separate mixtures to their bowls and add ½ cup of the white chocolate pistoles to each bowl. Using a rubber spatula, mix the chocolate and cream until the chocolate has completely melted into a smooth consistency. Serve immediately or keep at room temperature for up to about 1 hour.

To serve:

On a large serving tray, arrange the paintbrush cookies in a clean tin can or a pencil holder or cylinder to suggest paintbrushes in an artist's studio. Place the bowls of colored chocolate ganache on the tray like little pots of paint. For added effect, you can dip the ends of some of the cookies into the bowls of colored chocolate. Drizzle and drip a few of the colors on the brush container and the serving tray as if paint has dripped by accident from the brushes. Allow your guests to choose brushes from the container and dip them in their choice of chocolate ganache.

MERINGUE TOY BOX

Perfect for a baby shower or kid's birthday celebration, these colorful meringues are surprisingly easy to make. They are also a great, sweet alternative to really heavy desserts. Toy stores offer endless inspiration for recipe presentations and serving props.

We baked these whimsical shapes directly onto long wooden skewers like lollipops so that we could arrange them easily into the toy box pictured. You could also pipe out flower shapes onto the skewers and arrange them like flowers in a vase. Or, you can skip the skewers and serve the meringues on a cookie tray.

Serves 10 to 12

SPECIAL EQUIPMENT
- **24 to 36 wooden skewers**

- **8 large egg whites**
- **½ teaspoon table salt**
- **½ teaspoon cream of tartar**
- **2 cups plus 1 tablespoon granulated sugar**
- **4 different food colorings of choice**

Preheat the oven to 225°F. Line two baking sheets with parchment paper and lay wooden skewers ½ inch apart on the parchment.

Combine the egg whites, salt, and cream of tartar in the bowl of a stand mixer fitted with the whisk attachment. Beat on medium speed until soft peaks form. With the mixer on low, gradually add the sugar and continue beating until stiff peaks are formed.

Divide the egg white mixture evenly among four separate bowls and add a few drops of food coloring to each bowl, using a different color in each. Stir gently until, desired color is achieved. Transfer the mixtures to four separate piping bags fitted with large star and round tips, then pipe out different shapes on top of the skewers.

Bake the meringues for 1½ hours or until completely dry. Allow the meringues to cool completely and store in a perfectly dry, airtight container for up to 2 days.

continued

CHINESE CHECKERS TRUFFLES

Board games, by their nature, bring people together. They are created with fun colors and shapes to stimulate the eye. Chinese checkers is a classic that is immediately identified by its star-shaped board and colorful marbles. Choose your strategy, make a move, and pop your game piece into your mouth.

Note: *There are wonderful vintage Chinese checkers boards available on Etsy or eBay. Scour local yard sales and thrift stores, or head to the local toy store to get a brand new one.*

Makes 60 to 80 truffles

SPECIAL EQUIPMENT
- **Chinese checkers board**

- **1 teaspoon grated peeled fresh ginger**
- **¼ teaspoon ground white pepper**
- **¼ teaspoon cayenne pepper**
- **¼ teaspoon ground cinnamon**
- **¼ teaspoon ground cloves**
- **¼ teaspoon ground star anise**
- **¾ cup heavy whipping cream**
- **24 ounces bittersweet chocolate, coarsely chopped**
- **4 tablespoons (½ stick) unsalted butter, at room temperature**
- **Powdered food coloring in 6 different bright colors (bright colors are available online and at craft stores and cake decorating supply stores)**

Place the grated ginger, white pepper, cayenne pepper, cinnamon, cloves, and star anise in their own individual small bowls.

Heat the heavy cream in a medium saucepan over medium-high heat just until it simmers. Pour 2 tablespoons of cream into each of the spice bowls. Cover and steep at room temperature for 30 minutes. Strain each mixture separately through a fine-mesh sieve into separate bowls.

Place the chopped chocolate in a medium heatproof mixing bowl. Heat 1 inch of water in a medium saucepan over low heat until it simmers. Set the bowl of chocolate over the simmering water. (The bottom of the bowl should not touch the water.) Stir until the chocolate melts completely. Once melted, divide the chocolate among the six bowls of infused cream and stir until smooth and shiny. Cool completely.

Place the food colorings in separate small bowls.

Use a teaspoon to scoop and shape the chocolate into ½-inch balls that will fit into the Chinese checkers board. Roll each flavor of truffle in a different powdered food coloring and serve on the Chinese checkers board.

BEWARE— THIS COMES WITH A KICK

4

GROWN-UP SLIDERS

These decadent sliders make terrific heavy hors d'oeuvres for entertaining. Three of them together make a meal. The idea here is to take an iconic casual food and make it elegant by using the best sushi-grade tuna, caviar, Kobe beef, and truffles. You may want to let your friends know that this is a "slider" party but make sure you set a formal dress code.

Note: *Look for the foie gras, sevruga caviar, and black summer truffles at specialty gourmet markets and online. You'll need a 3-inch round biscuit cutter to cut out the slider biscuits.*

SLIDER BUTTERMILK BISCUITS

Makes 8 (double this recipe if preparing both the tuna and Kobe sliders)

- **2 cups all-purpose flour, plus extra for dusting**
- **1 tablespoon baking powder**
- **¼ teaspoon baking soda**
- **¾ teaspoon table salt**
- **2 tablespoons unsalted butter, chilled**
- **2 tablespoons vegetable shortening**
- **1 cup buttermilk**
- **1 large egg, lightly beaten**
- **1 teaspoon sesame seeds for the tuna sliders or white truffle oil for the Kobe sliders**
- **1 teaspoon wasabi powder for the tuna sliders or chopped truffles for the Kobe sliders**

Preheat the oven to 450°F.

In the bowl of a food processor, combine the flour, baking powder, baking soda, and salt. Add the cold butter and shortening and pulse until the mixture looks like crumbs. With the food processor running, add the buttermilk. Mix just until the dough comes together. The dough will be very sticky.

Turn the dough out onto a lightly floured surface. Fold the dough over on itself 5 or 6 times. Roll out the dough with a lightly floured rolling pin to about a 1-inch thickness. Cut out biscuits using a floured 3-inch round cutter. Place the biscuits on an ungreased baking sheet about 1 inch apart. With a pastry brush, lightly paint the top of the biscuits with the beaten egg. Sprinkle sesame seeds and wasabi powder on the top if making tuna sliders or brush with truffle oil and sprinkle chopped truffles on top if making Kobe sliders. Bake the biscuits until they are light gold on top, 18 to 20 minutes. Loosen the biscuits from the pan and wrap with foil to keep warm until ready to assemble the sliders.

continued

GINGER-LACED TUNA CRUDO SLIDERS WITH CAVIAR AND WASABI CREAM

Makes 8

TUNA CRUDO

- **1 pound sushi-grade tuna**
- **3 garlic cloves, minced**
- **½ teaspoon grated peeled fresh ginger**
- **2 teaspoons extra-virgin olive oil**
- **2 teaspoons toasted sesame oil**
- **2 tablespoons pickled ginger juice (drained from the jar)**
- **1 tablespoon soy sauce**
- **1 tablespoon sweet soy sauce**
- **1 tablespoon minced fresh chives**
- **1 teaspoon minced fresh cilantro**
- **1 teaspoon minced fresh basil**
- **1 teaspoon red pepper flakes**
- **1 tablespoon orange zest**
- **1 teaspoon table salt**

WASABI CREAM

- **1 cup crème fraîche (or sour cream)**
- **⅓ cup mayonnaise**
- **2 teaspoons wasabi paste**
- **1 teaspoon pickled ginger juice (drained from the jar)**
- **1 teaspoon fresh lime juice**
- **¼ teaspoon Chinese five spice powder**
- **¼ teaspoon toasted and ground coriander seed**
- **2 tablespoons chopped cilantro**

FOR SERVING

- **1 English cucumber, thinly sliced crosswise**
- **2 ounces fine caviar (such as sevruga)**
- **8 Slider Buttermilk Biscuits (page 129)**

For the tuna crudo:
One hour prior to serving, cut the tuna into ¼-inch dice. In a chilled mixing bowl, combine the tuna with the garlic, ginger, olive oil, sesame oil, ginger juice, both soy sauces, chives, cilantro, basil, red pepper flakes, and orange zest. Cover and place in the refrigerator for about 1 hour.

Mold into 8 small patties, about 2½ inches in diameter and 1 inch thick, and chill in the refrigerator until ready to use.

For the wasabi cream:
Combine all the ingredients in a mixing bowl and whisk until well combined. Refrigerate, covered, for up to 2 days.

To serve:
Split the buttermilk biscuits. Lightly toast the open-face side in a toaster oven or in a heated skillet. Let the biscuits cool slightly.

Spread the 8 bottom halves of the biscuits with some of the wasabi cream. Place a tuna crudo patty atop the wasabi cream, then top each patty with a dollop of caviar. Top each with a slice of cucumber and a biscuit top. Serve immediately.

KOBE BEEF SLIDERS WITH FOIE GRAS, SUMMER TRUFFLES, AND SMOKED BOURBON KETCHUP

Makes 8

KOBE BEEF PATTIES

- **1 pound ground Kobe beef sirloin (American Wagyu or Prime beef)**
- **4 tablespoons (½ stick) butter, at room temperature**
- **1½ teaspoons onion powder**
- **1½ teaspoons garlic powder**
- **4 green onions, minced**
- **¼ cup Major Grey's chutney, puréed**
- **1 teaspoon freshly cracked black pepper**
- **Sea salt**

SMOKED BOURBON KETCHUP

- **¾ cup ketchup**
- **⅓ cup bourbon, smoked (such as Maker's Mark bourbon smoked using mesquite chips), or alternatively seasoned with a dash of liquid smoke**
- **¼ cup pure maple syrup**
- **⅓ cup firmly packed dark brown sugar**
- **½ teaspoon table salt**

FOR SERVING

- **2 tablespoons white truffle oil**
- **2 slices havarti cheese, cut into quarters, making 8 small squares**
- **8 (1-ounce) slices foie gras**
- **2 small heirloom tomatoes, thinly sliced**
- **2 cups baby arugula leaves**
- **8 Slider Buttermilk Biscuits (page 129)**
- **Fresh sliced summer truffle (1 slice for each slider)**

For the Kobe beef patties:
One hour prior to serving, combine the ground beef, butter, onion powder, garlic powder, onions, chutney purée, and pepper in a chilled mixing bowl. Form into 8 small patties, about 2½ inches in diameter and 1 inch thick. Cover and store in the refrigerator for about 1 hour. When ready to cook, remove the patties and sprinkle with salt to taste.

For the ketchup:
Combine all ingredients in a small saucepan. Bring to a simmer over medium-high heat and whisk until the sugar is dissolved.

To serve:
On an oiled, preheated barbecue grill, sear the burgers for 3 minutes on one side. Flip and cook the other side for 1 minute. Drizzle the burgers with truffle oil, and top with the sliced havarti cheese. Cook until the cheese is melted and the burgers are just warm in the center.

Heat a skillet over high heat until very hot. Drop the foie gras slices into the dry pan, and sear on one side until golden.

Split the buttermilk biscuits. Lightly toast the open-face side in a toaster oven or on the grill. Let the biscuits cool slightly.

Top the biscuit bottoms with the hot burgers and foie gras. Top with a dollop of Smoked Bourbon Ketchup. Serve with sliced heirloom tomatoes and arugula leaves. Cover with biscuit tops, and place a truffle slice on top of each biscuit. Serve immediately.

IS YOUR
IMAGINATION.

frittata

ciego

chilaquiles

MEXICAN BREAKFAST

The bright flavors and colorful presentation of this menu make it a delicious alternative to more traditional brunch fare. Each dish is substantial on its own and easy to serve straight from the skillets or in individual servings. Three recipes here are interpretations of some traditional egg dishes. The frittata incorporates spicy chorizo sausage with bright pops of sweet cherry tomatoes. Chilaquiles, a sort of tortilla and chicken casserole, is also a wonderful dish to serve for dinner, and ciego is our upscale take on "toad in the hole."

FRITTATA

Serves 8

- **6 large eggs**
- **½ cup milk**
- **1½ cups shredded pepper Jack cheese (about 12 ounces), divided**
- **¼ pound fresh chorizo, crumbled**
- **1½ cups baby spinach**
- **2 cups halved cherry tomatoes**
- **1½ cups chopped green onions (white and light green parts only), divided**
- **1 cup sliced baby bell peppers, divided**

Preheat the oven to 375°F.

Whisk the eggs and milk together in a small mixing bowl. Stir in 1 cup of the shredded cheese. Set aside.

Place the chorizo in a 10-inch cast-iron skillet or other oven-safe skillet and sauté over medium-high heat until cooked through, about 5 minutes. Remove the chorizo from the pan, reserving the drippings in the pan. Add the spinach and sauté just until wilted. Add the tomatoes, half the onions, and half the bell peppers and continue to cook for 1 to 2 minutes or until the onions are beginning to turn translucent. Remove from the heat. Add the egg mixture and stir just until combined. Top with the remaining ½ cup shredded cheese.

Bake for 25 minutes or until a knife inserted in the center comes out clean. Remove from the oven and cool for 5 to 10 minutes. Slice into wedges to serve, garnished with remaining onions and peppers.

continued

CHILAQUILES

Serves 8

Note: *You'll need to make the Quick Tomato Sauce (see recipe below) before starting the chilaquiles. The cooked, shredded chicken is coated in the piquant sauce before layering with crisp corn tortillas and cheese and baking in the oven.*

QUICK TOMATO SAUCE

- **1 tablespoon olive oil**
- **1 large onion, finely chopped**
- **1 garlic clove, minced**
- **1 poblano pepper, seeded and chopped**
- **¼ cup finely chopped bell pepper**
- **12 Roma tomatoes, peeled, seeded, and chopped**
- **1 tablespoon chopped fresh cilantro**
- **Kosher salt**
- **Freshly ground black pepper**
- **Hot sauce, such as Tabasco**

- **4 (4- to 6-ounce) boneless, skinless chicken breasts**
- **1 onion, quartered**
- **2 garlic cloves**
- **Pinch of sea salt**
- **Quick Tomato Sauce (see recipe below)**
- **5 (8-inch round) corn tortillas, fried until crisp**
- **8 ounces Manchego cheese, thinly sliced**
- **8 ounces mozzarella cheese, thinly sliced**
- **8 large eggs, fried individually just before serving the chilaquiles**
- **½ cup sour cream**
- **¼ cup grated Cotija cheese**
- **Fresh cilantro sprigs**
- **Tortilla strips or crumbled tortilla chips**
- **Sliced baby bell peppers**

Make the tomato sauce:

Heat the olive oil in a medium saucepan over medium heat until it shimmers. Add the onion, garlic, and peppers and cook until the onion is translucent. Add the tomatoes and cilantro and cook for 10 minutes. Season with salt, black pepper, and hot sauce as desired. Keep hot while you prepare the chilaquiles.

Preheat the oven to 375°F.

In a 4-quart saucepan, combine 4 cups water with the onion, garlic, and salt. Bring to a simmer over high heat. Add the chicken and cook until the chicken is just cooked through, 8 to 10 minutes. Remove the chicken from the water and set aside until cool enough to handle. Shred the chicken into small pieces with your fingers or a fork. Add the chicken to the tomato sauce in the pan and stir to combine.

In an 8 x 8-inch glass baking dish, assemble the chilaquiles like a lasagna, starting with a layer of the fried tortillas, then the shredded chicken, and finishing with a layer of the Manchego and mozzarella cheeses. Repeat the layers until all the ingredients are used.

Bake in the oven for 30 minutes or until bubbly. Cool for 30 minutes.

To serve, place a scoop of the chilaquiles into each of eight serving bowls. Top each serving with a freshly fried egg and some of the sour cream, Cotija cheese, cilantro, fried tortilla strips, and sliced peppers.

CIEGO

Serves 8

- **8 tablespoons (1 stick) unsalted butter, divided**
- **8 (1-inch-thick) slices brioche, cut into 4-inch rounds with a 1-inch hole cut out of the center**
- **8 eggs**
- **1 cup Mashed Yukon Gold Potatoes (page 34)**
- **6 slices bacon, cooked and crumbled**
- **⅔ cup crumbled feta cheese**
- **⅓ cup thinly sliced sundried tomatoes**
- **2 green onions, thinly sliced**

Preheat the oven to 225°F. Line a rimmed baking sheet with parchment paper.

Melt 2 to 3 tablespoons of the butter in a large sauté pan over medium heat. Add 2 of the brioche rounds and cook until golden brown on one side. Turn the bread over and crack an egg into the center of each round. Cook for 2 to 3 minutes or until the egg is set but still sunny-side up. Carefully transfer the ciego to the prepared baking sheet and hold in the oven while cooking the remaining brioche and eggs.

To serve, place 2 tablespoons of the potatoes on each of 8 serving plates. Top with the ciego and garnish each serving with some of the bacon, feta, sundried tomatoes, and green onions.

WHY SERVE  ONE WHEN YOU CAN SERVE TEN?

TWISTED SISTERS

A mixed-up, rock-and-roll take on the ofttimes boring breadstick. I love the way sprinkling just one side of the dough with cheese, poppy seeds, and sesame seeds before twisting creates visual and textural interest. These are so easy to make and because they are textured, long, and twisted, it's fun to serve them in unconventional containers like cans, cylinders, and vases.

Makes 20 breadsticks

- ¼ cup grated Parmesan cheese
- ¼ teaspoon cayenne pepper
- ¼ teaspoon paprika
- All-purpose flour, for dusting
- 1 (7-ounce) package frozen puff pastry, cold but thawed
- 1 large egg, lightly beaten
- Pinch of coarse sea salt
- ¼ teaspoon poppy seeds
- ¼ teaspoon white sesame seeds

Preheat the oven to 425°F. Line a rimmed baking sheet with parchment paper and set aside.

In a small mixing bowl, combine the Parmesan, cayenne pepper, and paprika.

On a lightly floured surface, unroll 1 sheet of puff pastry and pat until flat and even. Lightly brush the surface with some of the egg. Let dry for 5 minutes or until it becomes tacky to the touch. Lightly sprinkle with half of the cheese-spice mixture, brushing off excess with a pastry brush. Carefully turn the dough over and repeat with some of the egg wash and remaining cheese-spice mixture. Transfer to a tray lined with parchment paper and chill in the refrigerator. Repeat the procedure on a second sheet of puff pastry, using poppy seeds on one side of the dough and sesame seeds on the other.

continued

Working with 1 piece of dough at a time, with the long side of the dough facing you, cut strips of dough about 1 inch wide. Transfer the strips to the prepared baking sheet, spacing them about 1 inch apart. Working with 1 strip at a time, hold each end with your fingers and carefully twist in opposite directions, forming a spiral. Press the ends of the strips against the parchment so they will not unravel.

Place in the freezer for 15 minutes before baking. Bake for 12 to 14 minutes, rotating the baking sheet halfway through, until golden brown. Transfer the breadsticks to a rack and cool for 5 minutes. While still warm, trim the ends of each stick with a knife to give them a clean look. When completely cool, store in an airtight container.

CEVICHE COCKTAILS

Enjoying seafood with cocktails by the sea is one of life's great pleasures. That's the inspiration behind these "spirited" cocktails. The first is a straight-up cocktail whose floral and citrus notes are designed to complement the flavors of seafood. We like to serve it alongside crackers topped with sushi-grade tuna and uni, as shown in the photo opposite. In the other recipes here, seafood and cocktail are merged together in one elegant serving. These are riffs on the classic Latin dish called ceviche, in which raw seafood is marinated in a citrus dressing, except here we are spiking the dressing so you can enjoy your ceviche with a kick.

MELON-GRASS FIZZLE

Makes 2 cocktails

FROZEN OPAL BASIL BOUILLON

- 6 tablespoons honey
- 2 teaspoons minced lemongrass
- Zest of 1 orange
- About ¼ teaspoon saffron
- 1 cup petite opal basil leaves

MELON CONSOMMÉ

- 1 cantaloupe, peeled, seeded, and coarsely chopped
- ¼ cup honey
- 1 (¼-inch) piece fresh ginger, smashed
- 2 stalks lemongrass, chopped
- ¼ cup freshly squeezed lemon juice
- 1 basil sprig
- 1 mint sprig
- 1 cinnamon stick

THE COCKTAIL

- 6 opal basil leaves, torn, plus more for garnish
- 6 mint leaves, torn, plus more for garnish
- 4 ounces aged spiced rum
- ½ cup Prosecco or rosé sparkling wine

To make the opal basil bouillon:
Combine 4 cups of water with the honey, lemongrass, orange zest, and saffron in a large saucepan. Bring to a boil and cook until the liquid is reduced by half. Remove from the heat, cool slightly, and add half of the basil leaves. Cover and steep for 10 minutes. Cool completely and pass through a fine strainer into a pitcher or measuring cup with a pouring spout. Fill a mini square ice cube tray, with cubes ¾-inch square, with the basil bouillon. Place the remaining opal basil leaves into the bouillon and freeze.

For the melon consommé:
Combine ½ cup of water with the cantaloupe, honey, ginger, and lemongrass in a blender. Blend on high until smooth. Transfer the puree to a small saucepan, and add the lemon juice, basil, mint, and cinnamon. Place over low heat and bring to a simmer, until the pulp rises to the top. Simmer very slowly, until the liquid appears clear beneath the cloud of pulp. Carefully skim off the cloud of pulp, and strain the liquid through a cheesecloth. Transfer to the refrigerator and chill completely.

For the cocktail:
Place four opal basil bouillon cubes in a cocktail glass along with three torn opal basil leaves and three torn mint leaves. Top with 2 ounces of the rum and 2 ounces of the melon consommé. Pour the Prosecco into the glass until the liquid reaches about ½ inch from the lip of the glass. Garnish with more basil and mint. Repeat with another cocktail glass. Serve immediately.

continued

LOBSTER BLOODY MARY

- **2 cups V8 juice**
- **1 cup vodka**
- **½ cup olive brine (olive juice)**
- **¼ cup Worcestershire sauce**
- **¼ cup prepared horseradish**
- **2 tablespoons hot sauce, such as Tabasco**
- **½ teaspoon kosher salt**
- **¼ teaspoon freshly ground black pepper, plus extra for garnish**
- **20 ounces cooked lobster meat, finely diced**
- **8 pitted green olives, finely chopped**
- **4 celery ribs, tops intact and reserved for garnish, bottom half of each rib finely chopped**
- **1 tablespoon chopped fresh flat-leaf parsley, plus 4 sprigs for garnish**

Combine the V8, vodka, olive brine, Worcestershire sauce, horseradish, Tabasco, salt, and pepper in a blender and blend until combined.

Pour the dressing into a mixing bowl. Add the lobster meat, olives, chopped celery, and chopped parsley, and stir to combine.

Serve in clear glasses, such as beer flight glasses or martini glasses, and garnish each glass with a celery top, sprig of parsley, and grind of black pepper.

OYSTER WHITE RUSSIAN

- **12 fresh oysters on the half shell**
- **2 cups half-and-half**
- **2 cups Irish cream liqueur**
- **1 cup vodka**
- **¼ teaspoon kosher salt**
- **1 tablespoon finely chopped fresh chives**
- **Potato chips, for garnish**
- **Baby lettuce sprouts, for garnish**

Preheat the broiler.

Arrange the oysters on a rimmed baking sheet and broil for 3 to 6 minutes or until the oysters are just cooked through. Remove the oysters from their shells and chill in the refrigerator until cooled completely. Chop the oysters into bite-size pieces and return to the refrigerator.

Combine the half-and-half, Irish cream, vodka, and salt in a blender and blend until combined. Place the chilled oysters in a mixing bowl. Pour the dressing over the oysters, add the chives, and stir to combine. Cover and chill for 1 hour or serve immediately.

Serve in clear glasses, such as beer flight glasses or martini glasses, and garnish each serving with potato chips and baby lettuce sprouts.

SCALLOP COLADA

- **1 pound sea scallops, rinsed, drained, and abductor muscle removed**
- **1 tablespoon olive oil**
- **½ teaspoon kosher salt**
- **½ cup pineapple juice**
- **Zest of 2 limes**
- **Juice of 3 limes**
- **½ cup coconut milk**
- **½ cup Coco Lopez**
- **1 cup finely chopped fresh pine-apple**
- **½ cup grated fresh coconut**
- **2 tablespoons finely chopped red onion**
- **1 tablespoon finely chopped jalapeño**
- **4 cherries, for garnish**
- **Fresh mint leaves, for garnish**

Preheat the oven to 350°F.

Pat the scallops dry and transfer to a medium mixing bowl. Add the olive oil and salt and toss to coat the scallops. Arrange the scallops on a rimmed baking sheet and bake to medium doneness, 5 to 8 minutes. Chill the scallops in the refrigerator until cooled completely.

Once cool, dice the scallops into small pieces, transfer to a medium mixing bowl, and return to the refrigerator.

Combine the pineapple juice, lime zest, lime juice, coconut milk, and Coco Lopez in a blender and blend until combined. Pour the dressing over the scallops in the bowl, add the chopped fresh pineapple, fresh coconut, red onion, and jalapeño and stir to combine. Cover and refrigerate for 4 hours.

Serve in clear glasses, such as beer flight glasses or martini glasses, and garnish each glass with a cherry and some mint leaves.

CALAMARI TEQUILA

- **1½ pounds fresh calamari tubes and tentacles, rinsed and patted dry**
- **2½ cups pineapple juice**
- **½ cup freshly squeezed lime juice**
- **1 tablespoon minced fresh Fresno chile**
- **1 ounce chopped fresh cilantro, plus extra for garnish**
- **1 ounce chopped fresh mint, plus extra for garnish**
- **1 cup best-quality tequila**
- **1 ounce diced red onion**
- **1 ounce diced tomato**
- **1 ounce chopped fresh chives**
- **¾ cup olive oil**
- **1 teaspoon sea salt**

Cut the calamari tubes into small pieces and transfer to a medium mixing bowl. Reserve 6 to 8 single tentacles for garnish. Chop the remaining tentacles and transfer to the bowl with the tubes. Add all the remaining ingredients and stir to combine. Cover the ceviche and refrigerate for 4 hours.

For the garnish, bring a pot of salted water to a boil and cook the reserved tentacles for 55 seconds. Remove from the pot and toss with a tablespoon of the liquid from the ceviche.

Serve the ceviche in clear glasses, such as beer flight glasses or martini glasses, and garnish each glass with a tentacle as if it is crawling out of the glass.

POP SHOTS

These are not the shots you remember from college. Serious, well-balanced cocktails are transformed into elegant little one-bite jelly shots. Their colors and garnishes make them irresistible, so be careful—they pack a punch! This recipe is fun for folks who love a DIY project. For this recipe, you will need some unconventional equipment. Two PVC tubes lined with acetate will act as your molds for these treats. It works best to buy acetate in sheets and cut it to size to fit inside the tubes. Don't forget your safety goggles!

SPECIAL EQUIPMENT

- **2 (8-inch-long by 1-inch-wide) PVC tubes**
- **Acetate sheets (available at baking supply stores)**
- **Plastic wrap**
- **Duct tape or painter's tape**
- **Pan or cup filled with raw rice**
- **Funnel**

KAMIKAZE

Makes 6 individual "shots"

- **2 sheets gelatin**
- **5 tablespoons simple syrup**
- **¼ cup freshly squeezed lime juice**
- **1 teaspoon agar-agar powder**
- **¼ cup blue curaçao liqueur**
- **¼ cup vodka**
- **Peel of 1 lemon, cut into strips, for garnish**
- **Herb flowers, such as lavender, coriander blossoms, or tiny microgreens**

Line 1 PVC tube with a piece of acetate. Wrap one end of the tube with plastic wrap and secure with tape to make it watertight. Stand the tube up in a pan filled with rice and set in the refrigerator.

Place the gelatin sheets in a bowl of cool water and let sit until they soften, 3 to 5 minutes. When soft, squeeze out the excess water.

Combine the simple syrup, lime juice, and agar-agar in a small saucepan set over high heat and bring to a boil, stirring constantly. When it comes to a boil, remove from the heat and add the blue curaçao, vodka, and softened gelatin sheets. If there are any clumps, pour through a fine-mesh strainer.

Using a funnel, pour the liquid into the PVC tube and refrigerate until set, about 2 hours.

To serve, gently slide out the acetate sheet from the PVC tube and unroll the jelly shot. Cut it crosswise into 1½-inch-long sections and stand them up on a serving dish. Garnish each shot with a lemon strip and an herb flower.

continued

mojito

kamikaze

MOJITO

Makes 6 individual "shots"

- ¼ cup simple syrup
- ¼ cup freshly squeezed lime juice
- 6 tablespoons clear rum
- 1 teaspoon agar-agar powder
- 2 sheets gelatin
- 2 tablespoons soda water
- 6 fresh mint leaves, minced, plus additional tiny leaves for garnish
- 3 teaspoons granulated sugar

Line 1 PVC tube with a piece of acetate. Wrap one end of the tube with plastic wrap and secure with tape to make it watertight. Stand the tube up in a pan filled with rice (or candleholders) to keep upright, and set in the refrigerator.

Place the gelatin sheets in a bowl of cool water and let sit until they soften, 3 to 5 minutes. When soft, squeeze out the excess water.

Combine the simple syrup, lime juice, and agar-agar in a small saucepan set over high heat and bring to a boil, stirring constantly. When it comes to a boil, remove from the heat. Pour into a stainless-steel bowl that is set into a larger bowl filled with ice water. Add the rum, softened gelatin sheets, and soda water. If there are any clumps, pour through a fine-mesh strainer. Add the minced mint. Stir the mixture until it is cool to the touch.

Using a funnel, pour the liquid into the PVC tube and refrigerate until set, about 2 hours.

To serve, gently slide out the acetate sheet from the PVC tube and unroll the jelly shot. Cut it crosswise into 1½-inch-long sections and roll them in the sugar. Stand up the shots on a serving dish and garnish with tiny fresh mint leaves.

EACH DISH

SHOULD BE LIKE

EMBARKING UPON

A NEW ADVENTURE.

YOU HAVE TO

PLOT

YOUR OWN

COURSE.

SNOW CONE COCKTAILS

Carnival and amusement park food isn't just fun for kids. A snow cone on a hot summer day is a refreshing, nostalgic treat at any age. Small ice shaving machines are now available online and in department stores so we decided to make a grown-up version of snow cones using classic cocktails as our inspiration. You can serve these in small glasses (such as shot glasses or espresso cups) or in snow cone papers.

MANHATTAN

Makes 4 heaping 3-ounce servings

- **6 ounces simple syrup**
- **4 ounces whiskey**
- **2 ounces butter**
- **1 ounce sweet vermouth**
- **1 ounce dry vermouth**
- **Dash of Angostura bitters**
- **Fresh cherries, for garnish**

In a small saucepan over medium heat, cook the simple syrup, stirring frequently, until the syrup has the color and texture of caramel, about 12 minutes. Add the whiskey and butter and whisk until incorporated. Cool slightly and transfer the sweet whiskey sauce to a squeeze bottle.

Combine the vermouths, bitters, and ¼ cup water. Pour into ice cube trays and freeze until frozen, about 2 hours. When frozen, place the cubes into a snow cone machine and shave the ice into paper cones or shot glasses. Drizzle with the sweet whiskey sauce and garnish with a cherry.

continued

manhattan

martini

old-fashioned

MARTINI

Makes 4 heaping 3-ounce servings

- **3 ounces dry vermouth**
- **2 ounces simple syrup**
- **1 ounce olive brine (the juice from a jar of olives)**
- **6 ounces gin**
- **2 tablespoons freshly squeezed lemon juice**
- **Olives, for garnish**

Combine the vermouth, simple syrup, and olive brine. Pour into ice cube trays and freeze until frozen, about 2 hours. When frozen, place the cubes into a snow cone machine and shave into paper cones or shot glasses. Mix the gin with the lemon juice and drizzle over the shaved ice. Garnish with an olive.

MINT JULEP

Makes 4 heaping 3-ounce servings

- **6 teaspoons confectioners' sugar, divided**
- **½ tablespoon finely chopped fresh mint**
- **5 ounces bourbon**
- **Fresh mint sprigs, for garnish**

Mix 5 ounces water with 4 teaspoons of the powdered sugar and the chopped mint. Pour into ice cube trays and freeze until frozen, about 2 hours.

Mix the remaining 2 teaspoons sugar and the whiskey together and transfer to the refrigerator to chill. When ready to serve, place the mint julep ice cubes into a snow cone machine and shave into paper cones or shot glasses. Drizzle with the sweet whiskey mixture and garnish with a mint sprig.

SNOW CONE OLD-FASHIONED

Makes 4 heaping 3-ounce servings

- **2 ounces lemon-lime soda**
- **5 drops Angostura bitters**
- **½ ounce grenadine**
- **1 teaspoon granulated sugar**
- **1 ounce brandy**
- **Candied kumquats, for garnish**
- **Amarena cherries in syrup, for garnish (optional)**

Mix the soda with the bitters and grenadine. Pour into ice cube trays and freeze until frozen, about 2 hours. Mix the sugar with the brandy and transfer to the refrigerator to chill. When the old-fashioned ice cubes are frozen, place them into a snow cone machine and shave into paper cones or shot glasses. Drizzle the sweet brandy mixture over the shaved ice and garnish with the kumquats and cherries.

JAW-DROPPING CONSTRUCTIONS

"cheddar" cheesecake

blueberry cheesecake

feta cheesecake

biscotti toasts

CHEESECAKE BOARD WITH BISCOTTI

Trompe l'oeil means "to deceive the eye" in French. The term refers to a style of painting that makes us belive the painted objects are real. Similarly, this dessert is not exactly what it seems at first glance. It's really a collection of luscious cheesecakes and crisp biscotti cookies masquerading as a beautiful cheese course with crackers and dried fruits.

Serves 8 to 10

CHEESECAKES

- **Nonstick spray**
- **3 pounds cream cheese (six 8-ounce packages), at room temperature**
- **3 cups granulated sugar**
- **1½ cups sour cream**
- **6 large eggs, at room temperature**
- **¼ cup cornstarch**
- **¼ cup finely crumbled feta cheese**
- **Zest of 2 lemons**
- **Juice of 1 lemon**
- **Yellow food coloring**
- **Blue food coloring**
- **¼ cup blueberry jam**

BISCOTTI

- **1 tablespoon milk**
- **1 large egg**
- **1 teaspoon vanilla extract**
- **2 cups all-purpose flour, plus extra for rolling**
- **1 cup granulated sugar**
- **½ teaspoon baking soda**
- **½ teaspoon baking powder**
- **½ teaspoon table salt**

For the cheesecakes:

Preheat the oven to 250°F. Spray three 5-inch round cake pans with nonstick spray and set aside.

In the bowl of a stand mixer fitted with the paddle attachment, combine the cream cheese and sugar and beat until smooth. Add the sour cream and beat until smooth.

In a medium mixing bowl, whisk together the eggs and cornstarch until blended. Add to the cream cheese mixture and beat on high speed for 1 minute.

Divide the mixture among three separate mixing bowls. Add the feta to one bowl and stir to combine. Transfer the feta mixture to one of the prepared cake pans.

Add the lemon zest, juice, and a few drops of yellow food coloring to the second bowl and stir to combine. Transfer the lemon mixture to the second prepared pan.

In a small bowl, add 2 to 4 drops of blue food coloring to the blueberry jam. Pour half of the cheesecake mixture from the third bowl into the last of the prepared cake pans. Spread the jam evenly on top. Top with the remaining cheesecake batter, creating a middle layer of jam.

continued

GARNISHES
- **Grapes**
- **Assortment of dried fruit, such as apricots, figs, and plums**
- **Dates**
- **Nutes**
- **Preserves**

Place the filled cake pans in a large high-sided roasting pan filled a quarter of the way with boiling water to create a water bath. Bake for 1½ hours or until the cakes jiggle slightly in the center but not around the sides. Cool in the pans set on a rack for 30 minutes. Run a small sharp knife around the edges of the pans and cool completely in the pans before removing and serving.

For the biscotti:
Preheat the oven to 350°F. Line a rimmed baking sheet with parchment paper.

In a small bowl, whisk together the milk, egg, and vanilla.

In the bowl of a stand mixer fitted with the paddle attachment, combine the flour, sugar, baking soda, baking powder, and salt and beat on low speed just to blend. With the mixer on low speed, gradually add the egg mixture and beat until a dough forms. Using floured hands, divide the dough in half. Transfer the dough to a lightly floured surface and roll each half into a log that is 10 inches long and 2 inches wide. Transfer the logs to the prepared baking sheet, spacing them about 3 inches apart. Bake for 35 minutes or until firm to the touch. Remove from the oven to a cooling rack and cool for 10 minutes.

Reduce the oven temperature to 300°F.

Transfer the logs to a cutting board and cut them crosswise on an angle into ¼-inch slices. Return the slices to the parchment-lined baking sheet and bake for 5 minutes. Turn the biscotti over and bake for another 5 minutes or until they are light golden brown. While still warm, loosen each biscotti slightly and then cool completely in the pan. Remove from the pan when cool and store in an airtight container.

To assemble and serve:
Select a beautiful wooden board, piece of slate, or other serving tray on which you might typically serve a selection of cheeses. Carefully transfer the cheesecakes to the board, spacing them apart to leave room for your garnishes. Cut small or individual wedges and slices from 1 or 2 of the cheesecakes to give the impression that the party has already started. Artfully arrange your fresh and dried fruits, the biscotti "bread," and any nuts or preserves that might make your cheese board look authentic. Place appropriate spreaders or cheese knives on the board or lodged into the cheesecakes for guests to use to serve themselves.

SWEET NACHOS

Fool your friends with this plate of "nachos" at the end of a meal: the salsa, ground beef, and guacamole are really a fresh strawberry relish, chopped chocolate, and pistachio cream layered atop sugar-dusted fried wontons. Quietly chuckle to yourself as they first decline your strangely timed snack and then dig in when they realize that it is actually dessert?

Serves 4

MANGO "CHEESE"

- **2 cups heavy whipping cream**
- **1 cup thawed frozen mango purée (available online or in Latin food stores)**
- **1 drop of yellow food coloring**
- **¼ teaspoon vanilla extract**

In the bowl of a stand mixer fitted with the whisk attachment, whip the heavy cream until medium-stiff peaks form, about 5 minutes. Reduce the speed to low and gently mix in the yellow food coloring and the vanilla until blended. Cover and keep refrigerated for up to 1 hour before serving.

PISTACHIO GUACAMOLE

- **1 quart heavy whipping cream**
- **1 tablespoon confectioners' sugar**
- **1 tablespoon pistachio paste (available online)**
- **1 drop of ivory food coloring**
- **1 drop of yellow food coloring**
- **2 tablespoons chopped fresh strawberries**
- **1 teaspoon chopped fresh mint**

In the bowl of a stand mixer fitted with the whisk attachment, whip together the heavy cream and confectioners' sugar until medium-stiff peaks form.

Using a spatula, fold the pistachio paste and both food colorings into the whipped cream. Fold in the chopped strawberries and mint until blended. Cover and keep refrigerated for up to 1 hour before serving.

continued

STRAWBERRY PICO DE GALLO

- **1 cup finely diced fresh strawberries**
- **1 tablespoon granulated sugar**
- **½ teaspoon freshly squeezed lemon juice**
- **1 tablespoon chopped fresh mint, plus more for garnish**

Combine all the ingredients in a small mixing bowl. Set aside or cover and refrigerate for up to 2 hours before serving.

SWEET SOUR CREAM

- **2 cups heavy whipping cream**
- **2 tablespoons confectioners' sugar**
- **¼ cup plain yogurt**
- **½ teaspoon vanilla extract**

In the bowl of a stand mixer fitted with the whisk attachment, whip together the heavy cream and confectioners' sugar until medium-stiff peaks form, about 5 minutes.

Reduce the speed to the lowest setting and gently mix in the yogurt and vanilla. Cover and refrigerate for up to 1 hour before serving.

WONTON TORTILLA CHIPS

- **6 cups vegetable oil, for frying**
- **10 frozen small wonton rounds, cut into quarters**
- **¼ cup granulated sugar**
- **½ teaspoon ground cinnamon**

Heat the oil in a medium saucepan over medium-high heat until it reaches 325°F.

Fry the wonton quarters in the hot oil in batches, being careful not to overcrowd, until the wontons are golden brown and crispy. Using a slotted spoon, transfer the fried wontons to a plate lined with paper towels to absorb the excess oil.

Combine the sugar and cinnamon in a small bowl and sprinkle over the chips while they are still warm.

CHOCOLATE GROUND BEEF

- **1 cup finely chopped semisweet chocolate**

To assemble the nacho plate:
Arrange the fried wonton chips on a serving tray or plate. Drizzle the chips with the mango cheese, top with dollops of the pistachio guacamole, sprinkle with the chocolate ground beef, layer on the strawberry pico de gallo, and top with a dollop of the sweet sour cream and more pistachio guacamole. Garnish with the finely chopped mint and serve immediately.

BLACK FOREST TOADSTOOL

Perhaps no food elicits more excitement in its presentation than a whimsical cake design. While most fancy cakes require lots of practice to produce, this one takes time but it's not difficult. Chocolate and "green velvet" cakes are crumbled and layered with chocolate ganache and whipped cream (and sometimes we add a cherry filling too), then topped with crunchy meringue mushrooms. There's no slicing stress here—just dish out servings with a spoon. To complete the look, try to find a woodsy serving bowl (we found a stump-shaped one in a home décor store). You could also plate the cake on a long, wooden serving tray (look for free-form wooden bowls and trays at stores like Target) by filling it with the cake and brownie crumbles and topping with the meringue mushrooms to look like a fallen log.

Note: You'll want to assemble this not more than a couple hours before serving it, but making several of the components ahead of time will make it easy to put it together. The sponge cake and the brownie "soil" can be made a day ahead and stored, covered, until you are ready to assemble the cake. The meringue mushrooms may also be made ahead; just be sure to let them cool completely before transferring them to an airtight container. Any moisture will cause the mushrooms to become soggy and sticky.

Serves 6 to 8

EMERALD SPONGE CAKE

- **Nonstick cooking spray**
- **1½ cups granulated sugar**
- **½ cup (1 stick) unsalted butter, at room temperature**
- **2 large eggs, at room temperature**
- **2 tablespoons Dutch-process cocoa powder**
- **1 (2-ounce) bottle green food coloring**
- **2½ cups all-purpose flour**
- **1 teaspoon table salt**
- **1 cup buttermilk**
- **1 teaspoon vanilla extract**
- **1 teaspoon baking soda**
- **1 teaspoon white vinegar**

For the emerald sponge cake:
Preheat the oven to 300°F. Spray a 9 x 9-inch cake pan with nonstick spray.

In the bowl of a stand mixer fitted with the paddle attachment, beat together the sugar and butter on medium speed until light and fluffy, about 3 minutes. Add the eggs, one at a time, beating well after each addition.

Combine the cocoa powder, food coloring, and ¼ cup water in a small bowl and stir until a paste forms. Add this paste to the egg mixture and mix on low speed until incorporated, about 1 minute.

continued

BROWNIE "SOIL"
- **Nonstick cooking spray**
- **2 cups (4 sticks) unsalted butter**
- **1½ pounds (24 ounces) semisweet chocolate, chopped**
- **6 tablespoons strong-brewed espresso**
- **2 tablespoons vanilla extract**
- **1 cup all-purpose flour**
- **1 tablespoon baking powder**
- **1 teaspoon table salt**
- **6 large eggs**
- **2½ cups granulated sugar**
- **¾ cup semisweet chocolate chips**
- **½ cup walnut pieces**

MERINGUE MUSHROOMS
- **1 cup egg whites (from about 8 large eggs)**
- **½ teaspoon table salt**
- **½ teaspoons cream of tartar**
- **2 cups plus 1 tablespoon granulated sugar**
- **Cocoa powder, for dusting**

WHIPPED CREAM
- **2 cups heavy whipping cream**
- **2 tablespoons granulated sugar**
- **1 teaspoon vanilla extract**

CHOCOLATE GANACHE
- **8 ounces bittersweet chocolate, chopped**
- **1 cup heavy whipping cream**

CHOCOLATE BUTTERCREAM
- **½ cup (1 stick) unsalted butter, at room temperature**
- **1 cup confectioners' sugar**
- **1 tablespoon milk**

Sift together the flour and salt into a small bowl. In another bowl, combine the buttermilk and vanilla. With the mixer on low speed, alternate adding the flour mixture and the buttermilk mixture to the green batter mixture, scraping down the sides occasionally, just until incorporated.

Combine the baking soda and vinegar in a small bowl and fold into the batter using a rubber spatula.

Pour the batter into the prepared pan and bake for 30 minutes or until the center of the cake springs back when lightly pressed. Cool completely in the pan.

For the brownie "soil":
Preheat the oven to 350°F. Spray a 9 x 9-inch baking pan with nonstick spray.

In the top of a double boiler, melt together the butter and chopped semisweet chocolate, stirring occasionally, until smooth. Remove from the heat and allow to cool slightly. Add the espresso and vanilla to the melted chocolate and whisk to combine.

In a medium mixing bowl, sift together the flour, baking powder, and salt.

In the bowl of a stand mixer fitted with the paddle attachment, beat together the eggs and sugar on medium-high speed until pale yellow and thickened, about 4 minutes. Add the flour mixture and beat on low speed just until combined. Scrape down the sides of the bowl, add the melted chocolate mixture, and beat on medium speed until incorporated, about 1 minute. Gently stir in the chocolate chips and walnuts using a spoon or rubber spatula.

Transfer the batter to the prepared pan and bake for 1 hour or until the top is shiny and slightly cracked, the edges are set, and the center is still a bit jiggly. Cool completely in the pan before cutting into squares.

For the meringue mushrooms:
Preheat the oven to 225°F. Line two baking sheets with parchment paper and lay wooden skewers ½ inch apart on the parchment.

In the bowl of a stand mixer fitted with the whisk attachment, beat together the egg whites, salt, and cream of tartar on medium speed until soft peaks form. Reduce the speed to medium-low and gradually add the sugar. Continue beating until stiff peaks form.

Place a medium-size round tip into a pastry bag and fill the bag halfway with the egg whites. To make the meringue mushroom caps, squeeze out round mounds of meringue onto one of the prepared baking sheets, pulling the bag off to the side after forming each mound to avoid making peaks on the top. To make the meringue mushroom stems, press out a tiny bit of meringue onto the other sheet pan, and pull the bag straight up. They should resemble candy kisses. Dust the meringues lightly with cocoa powder using a small strainer or sifter. Bake for 1½ hours or until completely dry on the inside. Cool completely. (You can store the completely cooled meringues in an airtight container at room temperature.)

Note: *For a more natural look, make caps and stems in a variety of sizes. You can do this by using round tips in a few different sizes or by varying the pressure you use when squeezing out the meringue forms. You can also pipe out some free-form shapes that resemble lichen (as in the photo) to attach to the side of the "stump." Just pipe out some of the whipped egg white and use a small butter knife or icing spatula to flatten the forms out into flat "lichen."*

For the whipped cream:
Using a handheld electric mixer or a stand mixer fitted with the whisk attachment, whip together the heavy cream, sugar, and vanilla until medium peaks form.

For the ganache:
Put the chopped bittersweet chocolate in a medium heatproof mixing bowl. Heat the cream in a small saucepan over medium heat and bring just to a soft boil. Pour the cream over the chopped chocolate and let sit for 1 minute. Whisk until smooth. Measure out about ¼ cup of the ganache and reserve for the chocolate buttercream.

For the chocolate buttercream:
Using a hand-held electric mixer or a stand mixer fitted with the paddle attachment, beat the butter and reserved ¼ cup ganache together until blended. Slowly add the confectioners' sugar and scrape down the sides of the bowl. Continue mixing until completely blended and smooth (but not gooey). If the buttercream is too thick—like a paste or forming a ball—add 1 tablespoon of milk to smooth it out. Continue adding milk or cream in very small increments and beat until a smooth frosting is achieved.

To assemble and serve the cake:
Crumble some of the brownie soil into the serving bowl or tray. Drizzle some of the ganache over the crumbles and top with some of the whipped cream. Create another layer of soil, ganache, and whipped cream until you have 2 or 3 layers of that combination. (The amount you use will depend on how big your serving piece is.) Top with a final layer of crumbled brownie soil. Place some of the emerald sponge cake in a decorative way to mimic green moss. You can also place the emerald sponge around the outside of the serving dish.

To complete the meringue mushrooms, place dots of the chocolate buttercream directly onto the bottoms of each mushroom cap. Press a mushroom stem into each cap to create a full mushroom. Use a little more buttercream to stick the mushrooms into the cake and around the "stump." Dust the entire creation with cocoa powder.

To serve, use a big spoon to dig down into the "stump" to get all of the layers in one serving. Make sure to put some "moss" and a meringue mushroom on each plate!

GIANT S'MORES

As if making a giant marshmallow isn't enough to thrill your guests, we turn it out onto a board or serving platter, caramelize the surface (using a small kitchen or crème brûlée torch), and surround it with chocolate bars and graham crackers. Encourage folks to use them to dip into the warm, gooey filling of the toasted marshmallow.

Note: *You can find glucose syrup at cake decorating stores and online.*

Serves 6 to 8

- **Nonstick cooking spray**
- **2 cups confectioners' sugar, plus ½ cup for the pan**
- **¼ cup glucose syrup**
- **10 sheets gelatin**
- **4 egg whites**
- **Pinch table salt**
- **2 teaspoons vanilla extract**
- **½ cup cornstarch**
- **Hershey's chocolate bars**
- **Graham crackers**
- **Regular and mini marshmallows**

SPECIAL EQUIPMENT:

- **You will need a standard angel food cake pan or a small food-safe plastic pail that is about 6-inches tall and 5 inches in diameter across the top. If you use a pail, you will also need a 15-ounce food can (label removed and washed) that has not been opened. Using a container with a column in the middle allows the marshmallow to set properly.**

Spray an angel food cake pan or a plastic pail and soup can with nonstick spray and set aside.

Combine 2 cups of the confectioners' sugar, the glucose syrup, and ⅔ cup water in a large saucepan over medium-high heat. Cook, stirring, until the sugar is dissolved. Clip on a candy thermometer and cook until the mixture reaches 262°F and becomes a pourable syrup.

Meanwhile, put the gelatin sheets in a bowl and cover with cold water. Let sit until softened. Once soft, squeeze out the excess water.

Combine the egg whites and salt in the bowl of a stand mixer fitted with the whisk attachment and beat until soft peaks are formed. With the mixer on low, add the gelatin, and then gradually add the sugar syrup mixture. Add the vanilla, increase the speed to high, and beat for 10 to 12 minutes or until the mixture is very stiff and just slightly warm.

continued

Whisk the remaining ½ cup confectioners' sugar and the cornstarch together in a small bowl. Coat the sides, bottom, and middle post of the cake pan or pail and soup can thoroughly. Reserve the leftover sugar mixture.

Spoon the marshmallow mixture into the prepared pan and sprinkle thoroughly with the leftover sugar mixture. Let sit uncovered at room temperature for 4 to 6 hours or until set.

Turn the giant marshmallow out of the pan onto a large serving platter. Using a kitchen torch, caramelize the surface until deep golden brown all over. Serve with chocolate bars, graham crackers, and marshmallows.

CHOCOLATE TREASURE CAKE

This brownie cake really is a treasure. I enjoy combing through antique and home décor shops for interesting serving ideas, and a little decorative chest sparked an idea for a rich dessert. The cake is assembled inside the chest and placed on a large serving tray surrounded by chocolate gold coins and graham cracker "sand." A hand-drawn treasure map with burnt edges would also add to the scene. For maximum drama, present this to your guests wearing an eye patch or with a parrot on your shoulder. Talk like a pirate.

Note: A wooden chest found at a home décor store makes an authentic or more mature look for this dish, or you could use a toy pirate's chest for a kid's party. Make sure the box is clean; you can also line the chest with plastic if it is made from a porous or difficult-to-clean material.

Serves 4 to 6

BARTON G.'S BROWNIES

- **Nonstick cooking spray**
- **2 cups (4 sticks) unsalted butter**
- **1½ pounds (24 ounces) semisweet chocolate, chopped**
- **2 tablespoons vanilla extract**
- **6 tablespoons strong-brewed espresso, cooled**
- **1 cup all-purpose flour**
- **1 tablespoon baking powder**
- **1 teaspoon table salt**
- **6 large eggs**
- **2½ cups granulated sugar**
- **¾ cup semisweet chocolate chips**
- **1 cup chopped walnuts, toasted**

For the brownies:
Preheat the oven to 350°F. Spray a 9 x 9-inch baking pan with nonstick spray.

Melt the butter with the chopped semisweet chocolate in the top of a double boiler. Remove from the heat and let the chocolate mixture cool slightly. Add the vanilla and espresso to the melted chocolate and whisk to combine.

Sift together the flour, baking powder, and salt in a medium mixing bowl.

Combine the eggs and sugar in the bowl of a stand mixer fitted with the paddle attachment and beat on medium-high speed until pale yellow and thickened, about 4 minutes. Add the flour mixture and beat on low speed just until combined. Add the melted chocolate mixture and beat on medium speed until incorporated. Stir in the chocolate chips and walnuts.

continued

CHOCOLATE GANACHE SAUCE

- **9 ounces bittersweet chocolate, chopped**
- **1 cup heavy whipping cream**
- **1 tablespoon dark rum (optional)**

TO ASSEMBLE

- **1½ cups graham cracker crumbs, for serving**
- **Chocolate gold coins, for serving**
- **2 cups Vanilla Ice Cream (page 95), for serving**

Transfer the batter to the prepared pan and bake for 1 hour or until the top is shiny and slightly cracked, the edges are set, and the center is still a bit jiggly. Cool completely in the pan before cutting into squares. The size and shape of your squares will depend on what kind of "treasure chest" you are using. Feel free to estimate what size squares will fit into your treasure chest and cut to fit 2 to 4 squares inside. You can also stack them for a taller presentation.

For the chocolate ganache sauce:
Put the chopped chocolate in a medium heatproof mixing bowl. Heat the cream in a small saucepan over medium heat and bring just to a boil. Pour the hot cream over the chopped chocolate and let sit for 1 minute. Whisk until smooth. Stir in the rum, if desired, and serve warm.

To assemble and serve:
Place the treasure chest on a tray and then pile the ground graham cracker crumbs all around as if the chest has just been unearthed from the sand or dropped into the sand after being pulled from the ocean floor. Make the "sand" uneven and messy to look like a real sand dune or beach. Place the gold coins around the chest as if they have been dug out and hastily put into pockets—spilling all over the beach. Once you have your sandy landscape, assemble the brownie squares inside the treasure chest, sprinkling graham cracker crumbs under and around the brownies. Top with vanilla ice cream and the warm chocolate ganache sauce. Serve immediately.

RADA'S COOKIES

My grandmother Rada made incredible cookies—especially rugelach. She was generous with her treats and this collection of cookies is meant to be made in a large quantity and served in an overflowing manner that evokes endless comfort and hospitality.

RUGELACH

Makes 3 dozen

PASTRY
- 1 cup (2 sticks) unsalted butter, at room temperature
- 1 (8-ounce) package cream cheese, at room temperature
- ½ teaspoon table salt
- 2 large eggs, at room temperature
- 2 cups all-purpose flour, plus extra for rolling

FILLING
- 1 cup golden raisins
- ½ cup walnut pieces
- 3 cups granulated sugar, divided
- 1 teaspoon ground cinnamon
- ½ cup (1 stick) unsalted butter, melted
- 1 large egg
- ¼ cup milk

For the pastry:
Combine the butter, cream cheese, and salt in the bowl of a stand mixer fitted with the paddle attachment and beat until well combined and creamy. With the mixer on low, add the eggs, 1 at a time, beating until well combined after each addition. With the mixer on low, add the flour and beat just until combined. Shape the dough into a ball, wrap in plastic, and refrigerate for 2 hours or overnight.

Preheat the oven to 350°F. Line two rimmed baking sheets with parchment paper.

For the filling:
Combine the raisins, walnuts, 2 cups of the sugar, and cinnamon in a food processor and pulse until coarsely ground.

On a lightly floured surface, roll the dough out to about ¼-inch thickness and 14 inches in diameter. Cut the circle into 16 equal wedges. Brush the surface of each wedge with the melted butter and sprinkle the ground nut mixture over the top in an even layer.

Roll up each wedge, starting with the wide end. Place the cookies, with the points tucked under, onto the baking sheets, and refrigerate for 30 minutes.

Whisk the egg and milk together in a small bowl.

Brush each cookie with the egg wash, sprinkle with the remaining 1 cup of sugar, and bake for 15 to 20 minutes until cooked through and lightly brown. Transfer the cookies to a wire rack to cool. When completely cool, store the cookies in an airtight container.

continued

ARABIC COOKIES

Makes 2 dozen

- 3⅓ cups all-purpose flour, plus extra for rolling
- 1 tablespoon ground cardamom
- 2 tablespoons baking powder
- 1 cup (2 sticks) unsalted butter
- ½ cup light beer
- 1 cup confectioners' sugar

Preheat the oven to 325°F. Line two rimmed baking sheets with parchment paper.

In a large mixing bowl, sift together the flour, cardamom, and baking powder.

Bring the butter just to a boil in a small saucepan. Add the melted butter to the flour mixture and stir with a wooden spoon just until combined. Add the beer and stir until well combined. Cover the dough with a damp towel and let sit for 1 minute.

Turn the dough out onto a lightly floured surface and roll the dough to a 1-inch thickness. Cut the cookies out using a 2-inch round cookie cutter. Set the cookies 1 inch apart on the prepared baking sheets and bake for 30 minutes or until light golden brown. Transfer the cookies to a wire rack to cool. When completely cool, roll each cookie in the confectioners' sugar and store in an airtight container.

RASPBERRY THUMBPRINT COOKIES

Makes 2 dozen

- 2½ cups all-purpose flour, plus extra for rolling
- ½ cup cornstarch
- 1 cup (2 sticks) unsalted butter, at room temperature
- 1 cup confectioners' sugar
- 4 large egg yolks
- 1 cup finely ground walnuts
- 1 cup finely ground blanched almonds
- ¾ cup raspberry jam

Whisk together the flour and cornstarch in a small mixing bowl. Set aside.

Combine the butter and sugar in the bowl of a stand mixer fitted with the paddle attachment. Beat on medium speed until well combined. With the mixer on low, add the egg yolks, one at a time, beating until well combined after each addition. With the mixer on low, add the flour mixture and beat just until combined. Add the ground nuts and beat until combined.

Divide the dough into 4 equal portions and shape each portion into a disc. Wrap each disk in plastic wrap and refrigerate for 4 hours or until firm.

Preheat the oven to 325°F. Line two rimmed baking sheets with parchment paper.

On a lightly floured surface, working with one disc of dough at a time, roll out the dough to a ¼-inch thickness and cut out cookies using a 2-inch round cookie cutter. Set the cookies on the prepared baking sheets and make an indentation in the center of each using your thumb. Place a small amount of the raspberry jam in the indentation of each cookie and bake for 15 to 20 minutes or until light golden brown. Cool completely on a wire rack and store in an airtight container.

WE SEE THE KITCHEN
AS A
CONSTRUCTION SITE.
ANYTHING
AND
EVERYTHING
CAN BECOME A
BUILDING BLOCK.

GIANT CHOCOLATE "KISS KISS" CAKE

Instantly recognizable, the classic chocolate-kiss candy is transformed into a larger-than-life version that is packed with four kinds of chocolate flavor and texture. We found the large metal serving bowl that is in the photograph on page 187 and it instantly reminded us of a piece of foil wrapping that had been opened. You could also use a metal tray with a deep enough lip to hold the pool of chocolate crème anglaise that surrounds the cake. This cake is perfect for a celebration or a supersize way to give a kiss.

Serves 6 to 8

SPECIAL EQUIPMENT
- **One 9-inch cardboard cake round, available at bakery supply stores**

CHOCOLATE CAKE
- **3 cups all-purpose flour**
- **1½ cups unsweetened cocoa powder, not Dutch process**
- **1 tablespoon baking powder**
- **1½ teaspoons baking soda**
- **1 teaspoon table salt**
- **2 cups sour cream**
- **1 tablespoon vanilla extract**
- **2 cups (4 sticks) unsalted butter, at room temperature**
- **2½ cups firmly packed light brown sugar**
- **6 large eggs**

CHOCOLATE ICING
- **¾ cup (1½ sticks) unsalted butter, at room temperature**
- **1 cup whipped cream cheese**
- **4 ounces unsweetened chocolate, melted and cooled**
- **1 teaspoon vanilla extract**
- **2½ cups confectioners' sugar**

For the chocolate cake:

Preheat the oven to 350°F and grease and flour two 9-inch round cake pans and two 6-inch round cake pans.

In a medium mixing bowl, sift together the flour, cocoa powder, baking powder, baking soda, and salt. In a small mixing bowl, whisk together the sour cream, vanilla extract, and ⅔ cup water.

In the bowl of a stand mixer fitted with the paddle attachment, beat together the butter and sugar until light and fluffy, about 3 minutes. Add the eggs, one at a time, beating well after each addition. With the mixer on low speed, add the flour mixture to the butter mixture, alternating with the sour cream mixture, beginning and ending with the flour, beating until the batter is well blended.

Divide the batter among the prepared pans and bake for 25 to 30 minutes, or until the center of each cake springs back when lightly pressed. Cool the layers in the pans on a wire rack for 10 minutes before turning out onto the racks to cool completely.

For the chocolate icing:

In the bowl of a stand mixer fitted with the paddle attachment, beat together the butter and cream cheese until light and fluffy. Add the melted chocolate and vanilla and beat until well combined. Add the confectioners' sugar and beat until well combined and smooth.

continued

CHOCOLATE GANACHE

- **9 ounces bittersweet chocolate, chopped**
- **1 cup heavy whipping cream**
- **1 tablespoon dark rum (optional)**

CHOCOLATE CRÈME ANGLAISE

- **1½ cups whole milk**
- **¾ cup heavy whipping cream**
- **¼ cup granulated sugar**
- **4 large egg yolks, whisked**
- **4 ounces bittersweet chocolate, finely chopped**
- **1½ teaspoons vanilla extract**

For the chocolate ganache:

Place the chocolate in a medium mixing bowl. Heat the cream in a small saucepan over medium heat and bring just to a boil. Pour the cream over the chopped chocolate and let sit for 1 minute. Whisk until smooth. Stir in the rum, if desired.

For the chocolate crème anglaise:

In a small saucepan over medium heat, heat the milk, heavy cream, and sugar, stirring frequently, until the mixture simmers, about 8 minutes. Remove from the heat.

Put the egg yolks in a medium mixing bowl and whisk in the hot milk mixture by tablespoonfuls until you've added ½ cup (8 tablespoons), then return the mixture to the saucepan and whisk together. Cook over medium-low heat, stirring with a rubber spatula, until the custard reaches 160°F, and thickens enough to coat the back of a spoon, 5 to 8 minutes. Remove from the heat and whisk in the chocolate and vanilla until melted and smooth. Pour through a fine-mesh strainer into a bowl set over a larger bowl filled with ice water and stir frequently for 10 minutes or until the mixtures cools completely.

To assemble the cake:

Place one of the 9-inch cake layers on a 9-inch cardboard cake round that has been trimmed to fit the cake exactly. Spread the top of the cake layer with ¼ cup of the icing. Place the second 9-inch cake layer directly on top of the first and spread with ¼ cup more icing. Next, place one 6-inch cake layer centered on top of the two 9-inch layers and spread ⅛ cup of the icing on top. Place the second 6-inch cake layer directly on top of the stack and again, spread ⅛ cup of the icing on top. Refrigerate for 2 hours to make it easier to trim off the edges of the cake into a chocolate-kiss shape.

To carve the cake into a chocolate-kiss shape, place a wooden skewer in the center of the cake to use as a guide. Carve the cake with a serrated knife on an angle. The tip of your knife should follow the outer diameter of the bottom layer while the end of your knife should be at the top of the cake cutting all around from the center of the top layer on about a 60-degree angle. The cake should be a cone shape. Spread the rest of the chocolate icing all over the cake, making a smooth, even surface.

Set the cake on a wire cooling rack with a sheet pan underneath. Pour the slightly cooled ganache all over the cake and refrigerate for at least 1 hour before serving.

To serve:

Pour the chocolate crème anglaise on a large, rimmed serving platter or into a shallow serving bowl, creating a pool, and then carefully transfer the cake to the center of the platter. Serve any additional chocolate anglaise on the side.

CONVERSION CHART

All conversions are approximate.

WEIGHT CONVERSIONS

U.S./U.K.	Metric
½ oz	14 g
1 oz	28 g
1½ oz	43 g
2 oz	57 g
2½ oz	71 g
3 oz	85 g
3½ oz	100 g
4 oz	113 g
5 oz	142 g
6 oz	170 g
7 oz	200 g
8 oz	227 g
9 oz	255 g
10 oz	284 g
11 oz	312 g
12 oz	340 g
13 oz	368 g
14 oz	400 g
15 oz	425 g
1 lb	454 g

LIQUID CONVERSIONS

U.S.	Metric
1 tsp	5 ml
1 tbs	15 ml
2 tbs	30 ml
3 tbs	45 ml
¼ cup	60 ml
⅓ cup	75 ml
⅓ cup + 1 tbs	90 ml
⅓ cup + 2 tbs	100 ml
½ cup	120 ml
⅔ cup	150 ml
¾ cup	180 ml
¾ cup + 2 tbs	200 ml
1 cup	240 ml
1 cup + 2 tbs	275 ml
1¼ cups	300 ml
1⅓ cups	325 ml
1½ cups	350 ml
1⅔ cups	375 ml
1¾ cups	400 ml
1¾ cups + 2 tbs	450 ml
2 cups (1 pint)	475 ml
2½ cups	600 ml
3 cups	720 ml
4 cups (1 quart)	975 ml
(1,000 ml is 1 liter)	

OVEN TEMPERATURES

°F	°C	Gas Mark
250	120	½
275	140	1
300	150	2
325	165	3
350	180	4
375	190	5
400	200	6
425	220	7
450	230	8
475	240	9
500	260	10
550	290	Broil

INDEX

Page references in italic refer to illustrations.

First published in the United States of America in 2014
by Rizzoli International Publications, Inc.
300 Park Avenue South
New York, NY 10010
www.rizzoliusa.com

Supervising Producer: Jill Cohen, Jill Cohen & Associates
Photographer: Ed Anderson
Recipe testing, styling, writing: Angie Mosier
Senior Editor: Christopher Steighner, Rizzoli Publications
Senior Designer: Paul Kepple, Headcase Design
Design Associate: Ralph Geroni, Headcase Design

Thank you to the entire team at Barton G.

2014 2015 2016 2017 / 10 9 8 7 6 5 4 3 2 1

Distributed in the U.S. trade by Random House, New York

Printed in China

ISBN-13: 978-0-7893-2720-8

Library of Congress Control Number: 2013952896